FORM CRITICISM

A Selection of the Volumes in

THE STUDIES IN THEOLOGY SERIES

FORM CRITICISM
ITS VALUE AND LIMITATIONS

by

E. BASIL REDLICH, B.D.
Canon Theologian of Leicester

Author of *The Forgiveness of Sins* and *The Student's Introduction to the Synoptic Gospels*

DUCKWORTH
3 HENRIETTA STREET, LONDON, W.C.2

First published 1939
Reprinted 1948

Made and Printed in Great Britain by
Thomas Nelson and Sons Ltd Edinburgh

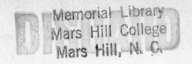
PREFACE

Form Criticism has been termed a " discipline," and so it is. As a method of investigation it is about twenty years old, and the exponents of the Form Critical school quite understandably overrate the value of their method, but there can be no doubt that *Form Criticism* has left its impress on the study of the Gospels. I have in this volume attempted to define the extent of this influence.

As far as possible, I have confined myself to references to books written in English, either as originals or as translations of German books.

Where quotations are made from the books marked with an asterisk in the bibliography (see page 199), the author's name alone is used.

Quotations from the Revised Version of the Bible are made by permission of the Syndics of the University Press.

E. Basil Redlich.

CONTENTS

CONTENTS

CHAPTER I

THE HISTORY OF FORM CRITICISM

FORM Criticism is a method of study and investigation which deals with the pre-literary stage of the Gospel tradition, when the material was handed down orally. It seeks to discover the origins and history of the material, that is to say, of the narratives and sayings which make up the Gospels, and to explain how the original narratives and sayings assumed their present form in the Gospels. It is concerned with the processes which led to the formation of the Gospels. It asks, for example, what the traditions were before they reached Mark, and to what extent, if any, he altered or adapted them; it asks whether his references to time and place were genuine, and whether he included matter which was current in the days in which he wrote his gospel and therefore could not have been primitive tradition.

According to the Form Critics, the evangelists were not authors, but collectors and editors. Their work consisted in collecting, choosing, grouping, re-shaping and handing down the traditions. They had nothing to do with the original moulding, for they took over material which had a " form " and which existed in independent self-contained units. Papias was in error in stating that " the evangelists were authors who shaped their narrative with literary freedom according to their knowledge of the events." As for these self-contained units, they obeyed certain laws, and to trace out these laws is to write the history of the Form of the Gospel. "The ultimate origin of the Form is primitive Christianity itself." This was the *Sitz im Leben* or Life-situation out of which the narratives and sayings sprang.

Form Criticism is a "literary-historical method." The term points to its association with the methods of investigation known as Literary Criticism and Historical Criticism. As to its connection with Literary Criticism, it accepts its main results, such as the priority of Mark, the existence of Q (the sayings—source common to Matthew and Luke), and would allow that special written sources were used by Matthew and Luke respectively. It is not therefore concerned with this literary problem of the sources of our written Gospels. But it is concerned to investigate the traditions as they really were before the Gospels or their sources were written, and to trace the influences which moulded these primitive traditions in the formative period, that is, before they received literary form. When Form Criticism first appeared its purpose was purely literary, "to introduce and establish a method of literary criticism." But it now has a wider scope. It has developed its technique and widened its range. It is now not a method of literary criticism but a literary-historical method.

By connecting itself with Historical Criticism, Form Criticism studies the narratives and sayings of other literatures, such as those of the Rabbis, Greece, Persia, India and China, in order that, by comparison with them, laws of tradition may be discovered and applied to the formation of the Gospel tradition. The forms of the independent units of the Gospel tradition, it is claimed, are like those assumed in folk-lore tradition, which were moulded by constant repetition.

But we must here insert a caveat. Historical Criticism must not be identified, as Form Critics often do, with the critic's own personal opinion of the historical truth of a narrative or saying. This latter is a historical value-judgment. It has no connection with laws of the tradition or with formal characteristics.

THE AIMS OF FORM CRITICISM

It is evident that, before the Gospels were written, there was a period of oral tradition when narratives and sayings of our Lord circulated by word of mouth. It is probable that in this period these narratives and sayings were subject to the usual inevitable fate of oral tradition, such as adaptation, alteration, and addition. Form Criticism claims that the laws of oral tradition can be discovered and stated, and that, by applying them to the Gospels, the narratives as they actually happened and the sayings as they were actually uttered by our Lord can be determined. This is one of the aims of Form Criticisim.

But there is a second and higher aim. In 1911 doubts were thrown in Germany on the existence of Jesus of Nazareth. It was even being denied that He really lived on earth. Form Criticism, it was hoped, would resolve this doubt. The method of Form Criticism, says Dibelius, a conservative Form Critic, " seeks to help in answering the historical questions as to the nature and trustworthiness of our knowledge of Jesus." Bultmann, one of the most sceptical of the Form Critics, concludes thus: "By no means are we at the mercy of those who doubt or deny that Jesus ever lived." In other words, the Form Critics claim that by their methods of investigation we shall know Jesus as He really was in the thoughts and minds of those who knew Him in the flesh, that we shall know the Jesus of history as He was before the Gospels were written, that is during the formative period. This we may be able to do by learning how the material was understood before it was included, after editing, in the Gospels. But to know Jesus as He was, we must get rid of all insertions and redactions due to the authors of the Gospels, and ask with what intention stories and sayings of Jesus were first collected and then written.

FORM AND VALUE-JUDGMENTS

The term Form Criticism is therefore a wider study than the mere investigation of the form or structures which the narratives and sayings gradually assumed during the oral period of transmission. The term in itself implies that its primary, if not its sole aim, is the discovery of the forms and style of the traditional material of the Gospels, that it is not to be confused with a historical valuation which determines whether the events narrated are true. By its designation Form Criticism should limit itself strictly to literary research as an extension of Literary Criticism. But the dual aim of Form Criticism shows that its purpose is not merely literary. If it seeks to know Jesus as He really was or even if He really lived, it must inevitably raise the question of the relation of the forms of tradition to history and investigate the truth of the narratives and sayings of the Gospel. We shall find that Form Critics claim that the forms assumed by the narratives and sayings as they were during the formative period are an index of their historicity. This is a reasonable piece of research. But when they proceed to give judgment on some narratives of Jesus which have no form or structure, then, indeed, we must make a protest and affirm that they go beyond their province, for it is purely historical and theological criticism without any reference to the forms of the original tradition.

Let us take a few illustrations. What was the concluding remark Jesus made to His mother and brethren when they came to fetch Him? Dibelius, who sees in this story, a " form " of narrative which was appropriate for preaching, holds that the answer of Jesus in Mark iii, 34, would have been sufficient for the situation, which concerned only His kins-folk. The words, " Behold, my mother and my brethren," are in keeping with the form. But for the purposes of preaching it was necessary to speak in a way which would appeal to the hearers of the sermon. Hence a sentence was added, whose historical truth must be doubted: " Whosoever shall do the will of God, the same is my brother and sister, and mother." A general principle was thus developed out of an isolated situation.

Another illustration of a similar kind is the Call of Levi. Jesus justified his action of calling a tax-gatherer with the words, " They that are whole have no need of a physician, but they that are sick." But for preaching, it was necessary to obtain from it " a doctrine "—" I came not to call the righteous, but sinners "—and this extra phrase was, in the early days of the Church, placed in the mouth of Jesus as a saying of His.

Whether we agree or not with the conclusions drawn by Dibelius, his treatment of the incident is in accordance with his method. He finds that certain narratives, useful for preaching, have a certain form, and he applies the characteristics of such form to these two narratives. This is real Form Criticism. How far these characteristics hold is another question, with which we shall deal later.

On the other hand, Dibelius, in dealing with another story of the class of narratives referred to, namely the story of the Sons of Zebedee, says that the words of Jesus to James and John about drinking the cup that He drank, etc. (Mark x, 38–40) are " evidently a *vaticinium ex eventu* which is bound up with the *pericope* for the purpose of glorifying the martyrdom of the two brothers that had already taken place." Dibelius may be right in his inference, but we hold that he is not dealing with Form Criticism but giving his personal judgment on the historical trustworthiness of Mark x, 38–40.

Let us take an illustration from Bultmann. In the incident of the Cornfields (Mark ii, 23-28) he states that the saying on the Sabbath (vv. 27 and 28) was originally an independent saying, but to it a narrative framework was attached by Christians to serve as an argument to justify their own attitude. He points out that in the narrative it is the disciples who are attacked. Had Jesus been attacked, says Bultmann, that would have given point to the whole incident. As that was not the case, the narrative and the saying are both unhistorical.

The incident is one of his group of Apothegms or narratives constructed according to certain laws of form. Bultmann's investigation is quite relevant, but, as we shall see later, his tests of genuineness are too subjective and he makes very little allowance for the creative genius of Jesus.

This distinction needs to be emphasized, for it is one of the weaknesses of Form Criticism that it confounds subjective historical judgment with Historical Criticism. If, for instance, these critics designate certain narratives as "Myths," they undoubtedly pre-judge their historical value. Further, according to their own admission, these particular mythical stories have no literary form and can only be classified according to their contents. Stories "without form" are beyond "Form" Criticism.

THE FORMATIVE PERIOD

One other preliminary remark must be made on Form Critical methods. Form Criticism is concerned with the oral period of the tradition. It may work backward from the written Gospels, irrespective of their written literary sources, and may also work forward from the life of the primitive community, that is from the life situation. How extensive this oral period was is problematic, for narratives were written before the first of our New Testament Gospels. If, as is possible, the written source common to Matthew and Luke, generally known as Q, could be dated about A.D. 50, and if the special source of Luke, designated L, was a document which could be dated about the same time, and if our Lord died about A.D. 30, the strictly oral period would be no more than twenty years. In point of fact, it is another weakness of Form Criticism that it sits too lightly on the results of literary criticism and assumes that the formative period lasted about two generations or forty years. Thus in their investigations there is a tendency to overlook the presence and influence of those who were eye-witnesses and ear-witnesses of the events of the life, death and resurrection of Jesus, and could therefore guarantee the historical value of the tradition.

THE POSITION BEFORE 1914

Form Criticism was born in Germany in the year after the close of the Great War of 1914–1918. In essentials, it is, as stated above, an extension or a growth from that form of the critical study of the sources of the Gospels known as Literary or Source Criticism. It arose from the inability of Literary Criticism to deal with problems associated with the pre-literary phase of the Gospels. It was not unexpected. A survey of the position in which the study of the Gospels was left just before 1914 will make this clear. For our purpose the outstanding scholars of the immediate pre-war age in Germany were Bernard Weiss, Holtzmann, Wrede, Johannes Weiss, Wellhausen, Gunkel and Wendling. Each of them in some way prepared the ground for the advent of Form Criticism, and before a student makes any attempt to understand this new branch of study, it is necessary that he should be aware of the contributions made and the questions raised, but left unsolved, by these distinguished German scholars in the field of Literary Criticism.

BERNARD WEISS (1901) carried on the work of

Carl Lachmann who in 1835 had proved from language alone that Mark was the primary gospel and was the basis of Matthew and Luke. But Lachmann's great contribution was overshadowed by Strauss who in the same year raised a more popular issue, for he denied the historical value of the Gospels. In his opinion they consisted of legends which were formed many years after the date of their supposed occurrence; the early Christian community attributed to Jesus what they thought He should have said and done. This is practically the standpoint of Bultmann, one of the modern Form Critics.

Bernard Weiss[1] countered the scepticism of Strauss. He supported Lachmann's theory that Matthew and Luke had a common source in Mark, and that Mark was therefore the primary gospel. The history of the ministry of Jesus ultimately depended on Mark. But was Mark reliable? As against Strauss, Weiss held that Mark's gospel gave a trustworthy outline of the ministry of our Lord and was historical. Did Matthew and Luke rely on any other written source and was this second source historical? Weiss answered that there was a second source used by Matthew and Luke, containing not only non-Marcan passages common to Matthew and Luke but also passages peculiar to Matthew and, in addition, a few Marcan passages. This source, now designated Q, was very reliable. Lastly, said Weiss, Luke used a third written source from which the evangelist obtained his special matter. Weiss called this source L.

HOLTZMANN (1901)[2] agreed with Weiss about the

---

[1] *Commentary on Mark and Luke.* [2] *The Synoptics.*

priority of Mark and the use of Q by Matthew and Luke, but he limited the contents of Q to the matter common to Matthew and Luke. As for the special source of Luke, it was not a document but consisted of oral tradition and Luke's own contribution, which he made by special editing of Matthæan matter.

These two scholars therefore gave us the " Two document hypothesis " of Literary Criticism. The synoptic problem of the similarities of the first three Gospels was amply explained by the theory that Matthew and Luke used Mark; the non-Marcan matter common to Matthew and Luke was due to their use of a second documentary source which was as reliable as Mark. These conclusions were drawn from an examination of the Gospels and not based on the well-known statement of Papias, but there is a remarkable correspondence between them.

Weiss and Holtzmann differed on the extent of Q. Modern scholars generally support Holtzmann's view of the contents of Q. But more important for the study of Form Criticism is the view of these two scholars that Mark is historical, and that a life of Christ could be written based on the chronological and biographical details given by the evangelist. This is known as " The Marcan hypothesis." No question was raised whether Mark had in any way interpreted any of the facts, as John had done so extensively in his Gospel. The Marcan hypothesis seems to most English students so fundamental, for without it no life of Christ can be written, that any attack which aims at undermining its stability is received with caution. But it is to doubts of the historical value of Mark that we ultimately owe the coming of Form Criticism.

WREDE (1901)[1] was the first German scholar who attacked the seeming impregnable citadel of Gospel study. His assault was made in three directions. First, he questioned the historical value of Mark and argued that Mark gave no reliable history of the ministry, for it was Mark who constructed the framework of the narrative. The contexts of the narratives and sayings were artificial. If Matthew and Luke, when they used Mark, adapted and altered the Marcan narrative, each with a special purpose in view, might not Mark have done the same with his sources? Wrede's answer was that Mark dealt as freely with the material as Matthew and Luke did. The historical background of Mark was therefore untrustworthy. Secondly, Wrede held that Mark was constructed from separate and independent narratives and sayings of our Lord, which were for the most part to be trusted for their accuracy. All the tradition, however, was not primitive. The evangelist inserted later tradition, later beliefs and practices of the Church, later observances and later views of the Person of Jesus Himself. Thirdly, Mark was written under the influence of a doctrinal theory which Wrede called " The Messianic Secret."

" THE MESSIANIC SECRET "

We had no right, argued Wrede, to assume that Mark gave us a true portrait of Jesus. What we find in his gospel is not a study of Jesus as He really was but as seen through the eyes of others.

The view hitherto accepted was that until Peter's confession the Messiahship was known only to

[1] *The Messianic Secret in the Gospels.*

Jesus, but that, as a result of the gradual training of the disciples, Peter discovered the secret. Henceforth it was known to them, but they were requested by Jesus to keep it a secret until after the Resurrection (Mark ix, 9-13). After the confession Jesus continued His training in order to enable the disciples to understand His own view of the Messiah, that the Messiah must first suffer and die.

This view Wrede would not accept. The disciples were not gradually educated to believe who He was, and the confession of Jesus as Messiah did not begin till after the Resurrection. This belief in the Messiahship was the outcome of the experiences of that event, which convinced the disciples that He was risen. The Messiahship was therefore not revealed to anyone during the ministry and the idea of it was not revealed to anyone before the Resurrection. Even Jesus did not believe He was the Messiah. What we find in Mark is a theory imposed by Mark on the narrative.

By his own theory Wrede explained what were to him serious difficulties in the Marcan gospel. In it there are passages which tell us that though demons recognized Jesus and proclaimed Him aloud as Messiah in the presence of people, men failed to recognize Him. Even the disciples failed to understand the Messiahship though they were repeatedly told of it. Mark attempted to explain this obtuseness by stating that the disciples were supernaturally prevented from realizing the truth (Mark vi, 52). In no other way can this curious phenomenon be explained than by assuming that Mark made Jesus a supernatural being recognized only by other supernatural beings, like the demons.

Some explanation is also needed for the frequent references in Mark to the imposition of secrecy by Jesus (i, 25, 34, 43 ; iii, 12 ; v, 43 ; vii, 24, 36 ; viii, 26, 30 ; ix, 9, 30) and to the many withdrawals of Jesus from the crowds in order to instruct the disciples (iv, 10, 34 ; vii, 17 ; ix, 28, 31, 33 ; xiii, 3). Mark is not to be relied on in passages about demons, the imposition of secrecy and the withdrawals. The only explanation of their presence in the Gospels is that belief in the Messiahship arose after the Resurrection, and then the life of Jesus was interpreted to mean that Jesus was conscious of His Messiahship from the beginning. The Marcan framework, says Wrede, was made in the interests of the theory of the Messianic secret and this hypothesis is supported by his belief that the original tradition circulated in independent units.

This theory of Wrede's is accepted by most of the Form Critical school, for example by Dibelius, Bultmann and R. H. Lightfoot. But the supporters of the theory have not fully faced the arguments on the other side, which may be stated as follows. Jesus might reasonably have Himself imposed the silence on His disciples because His view of the Messiahship was different from the popular view, and therefore could only be gradually unfolded to the disciples. Jesus Himself would naturally prefer to make the public announcement. As for the demons, it is possible that their recognition of Jesus was a theory of the evangelist. Mark held the knowledge of his own days on the sources and powers of the insane, and had he known something of the modern study of the psychology of insanity he would have explained demoniacal possession differently. Besides, if the insane did recognize Jesus, it is not impossible that the sane would consider what was said as the ravings of irresponsible persons and therefore *ipso facto* unreliable. Again, Jesus might have deliberately set Himself to check any attempt of the crowds to look upon Himself as a wonder-worker, and it is a fact that Mark does not use the miracle stories to prove the Messiahship, which he might have done had he imposed the theory on the tradition. Lastly, belief in the Resurrection might not necessarily have led to belief in the Messiahship, and no explanation has been given to explain how the Resurrection gave rise to the belief.

We may also add that Wrede does not explain how the Messianic secret became known to Mark, who himself did not originate it, nor whether the traditions and the secrecy existed together before Mark wrote his gospel.

The theory has been sympathetically and critically reviewed by Dr. Rawlinson in his *Gospel according to St. Mark* (pp. 258–262). We have made reference to it here, though it does not come within our subject, because it is assumed as proved by Form Critics in evaluating the contents of the forms.

JOHANNES WEISS (1903),[1] son of Bernard Weiss, answered Wrede's arguments by a careful and detailed study of Mark. He distinguished between primitive tradition and the evangelist's own contributions, and shewed that the Messianic consciousness of Jesus was not, as Wrede believed,

[1] *The Oldest Gospel.*

a creation of Mark but was a piece of authentic tradition. He was convinced that most of the Marcan material was historical, particularly those based on Peter's reminiscences, which affect about half the contents and include the Passion narrative. The sayings of Jesus from Q to be found in Mark were historical. On the other hand, he allowed that part of the material was not primitive but arose in the early Church, which sought the support of Jesus in controversial arguments with the Jews. He also admitted that some of the material was legendary. Yet in nearly all the Marcan material, whether original or edited by him, there was a foundation of fact.

WELLHAUSEN (1903)[1] laid down certain conclusions which shewed that he agreed with Wrede. Each of the Gospels is a collection of detached stories which were united by similarity of subject. Mark gives no chronology of the life of Jesus; its framework is artificial and made up of unhistorical editorial insertions. Mark contains good primitive tradition as well as views and teaching of the early Church, and the material of the gospel is influenced by the theology of the early Church. As for the source Q, which consists mainly of sayings, it too is of ecclesiastical origin, and gives no assurance of what Jesus taught and said.

Of other writers who contributed to the literary criticism of the Gospels before 1914, mention may be made of WENDLING[2] (1905) who held that there were two original sources in Mark, though badly united by him. These were Apothegms and

---

[1] *Gospel of St. Mark.*
[2] *Primitive Mark,*

Wonder-Stories, two well-known groups in Form Criticism.

We must also mention GUNKEL who had sought to discover the *Sitz im Leben* or the life-situation of the stories in Genesis. The application of this method of approach to the study of the Gospel stories was inevitable.

Hence in 1914, the position may be summarized as follows. The Two-document hypothesis was accepted, but the historical value of Mark and the trustworthiness of Q were being questioned. Secondly, it was being argued that Mark and Q were influenced by the theological views of the early Church. Thirdly, it was being asserted that Mark was a collection not only of traditional narratives and sayings of Jesus but of material of a later date. Fourthly, it was being said that Mark was not wholly based on the reminiscences of Peter but contained some legendary matter. Lastly, the presence of " forms " of oral tradition in Mark was being recognized.

Thus, the priority of Mark being accepted, attention was being concentrated on it. Questions were being asked which needed a reply. How was Mark written? What were his sources? Were his sources reliable? Was Mark influenced by doctrine as John was, though not to the same extent? Did Mark alter and adapt primitive tradition?

Form Criticism has been called by Vincent Taylor " the child of disappointment." There was much that Literary Criticism left unanswered concerning the pre-literary stage of the Gospels. But, further, questions were being asked of the pre-literary material, in addition to the problems associated with Mark. What was the nature of the narratives and sayings before they received literary form? What were the influences which led to their formation, transmission and preservation? What part did the community play in the stages of oral tradition? Do the forms of the tradition give any indication of their age and history? These are some of the questions which come up for consideration in Form Criticism.

AFTER 1918

The pioneers of Form Criticism were Dibelius,[1] Bultmann[2] and Schmidt.[3] Their first books appeared almost simultaneously in 1919, and yet they were working independently. They were on a similar quest, namely, the primitive tradition and the laws of their formation and transmission. We shall, in referring to the views of these writers, utilize their latest views in their later works.

K. L. SCHMIDT restated the old position very definitely and positively and carried out some investigations suggested by Wellhausen. The first step was an investigation of the editorial contributions of Mark. Schmidt's conclusions were to the following effect.

The framework of Mark is the work of the evangelist. The links in the gospel are mainly artificial and seldom historical. They are of no value chronologically, and of no use for a biographical outline of our Lord's life and ministry. The geographical details are not to be trusted, neither are the notes of time and place, such as " the house,"

---

[1] *The Form-History of the Gospel.*
[2] *The Criticism of the Synoptic Tradition.*
[3] *The Frame of the Story of Jesus.*

" in a boat," " by the sea-side," " in the synagogue."
These were obtained by Mark from purely internal
considerations. It is however allowable that the
names mentioned in the narratives are authentic.
Mark tried to bring some unity into his sources
by his own redactional insertions, which gave the
necessary background.

Mark's ministry of Jesus lasted one year.
Matthew and Luke altered the order and place of
events and therefore thought little of Mark's order.
Papias says Mark put down Peter's reminiscences
" but not in order." By recognizing how Matthew
and Luke dealt with Mark we can discover how Mark
dealt with his sources.

DIBELIUS is a conservative Form Critic. He is
also " constructive," for he does not work back
analytically from the texts of the Gospels to the
original traditions but investigates the life of the
early community in order to determine the relation
of the tradition to the conditions and activities of
the early Church. He is convinced, by the evidence
of the prologue to Luke's Gospel, that the traditions
received their form from the needs of missionary
preaching. By preaching he means all forms of
missionary propaganda, mission preaching, sermons
in worship and catechetical teaching. " In the
beginning was the sermon."

According to the Acts of the Apostles, the sermon
in early days had a settled plan. First came the
Kerygma or short message, then the proof from
scripture, and finally the call to repentance. The
first preachers did not preach about the life of Jesus
but the salvation which He wrought. Stories of
Jesus were used to illustrate and confirm this message

of salvation; they were of secondary importance. The aim of the sermon created the "form" of the story, and unliterary men thus created a definite style for propaganda. The normal unit was a short narrative which was valued for the saying, and not for the structure in which the saying was set. Everything in the story was subordinate to the saying, even though the narrative might include a miracle. Since each such unit was used as an illustration or model in preaching, Dibelius calls each of them a Paradigm. These Paradigms were originally independent of one another, and the preacher would choose them as he wished in order to support his theme. Mark however grouped them and edited some. There are only eight of these Paradigms in Mark which are of a pure form, and they can be easily separated from their contexts. These are the Sick of the Palsy, the Question of Fasting, the Ears of Corn, the Withered Hand, the Relatives of Jesus, Blessing the Children, the Tribute Money, and the Anointing in Bethany. There are ten other Paradigms but they are of a less pure type. Mark gives eight and Luke two. These ten are, the Unclean Spirit, the Call of Levi, Jesus in Nazareth, the Rich Young Man, the Sons of Zebedee, the Blind Man of Jericho, Cleansing the Temple, the Question of the Sadducees concerning the Resurrection, the Inhospitable Samaritans and the Man with the Dropsy. The last two are from Luke.

Everything in the Paradigms is concentrated on the saying. These model stories bore witness to the words of Jesus and hence in them are found the lack of portraiture, the brevity of the narrative, and the absence of artistic style. They arose in the early days when Christianity had not yet gone out into the secular world. There was nothing secular in tone in the narratives. This was the period of eyewitnesses and " such a date would guarantee a relatively high degree of historicity." Paradigms were the first to receive a definite form.

A second group is composed of stories about Jesus which set Him forth as a wonder-worker. Dibelius calls them Novellen or Tales. These were formed not for edification, not to show Christ's power over the human soul, but to display the power of Jesus over nature and sickness. They were valued for themselves and not for any saying in them, and might serve as examples to Christian healers and exorcists. They did not meet a religious need and were not used for Christian worship. There is a secular tone in them, and more is heard of secondary circumstances than in the Paradigms. They were the creation of a body of story-tellers.

There are ten of these Tales in Mark. The Cleansing of the Leper, the Stilling of the Tempest, the Gerasene demoniac, the Daughter of Jairus, the Woman with the Issue of Blood, the Feeding of the Five Thousand, the Walking on the Sea, the Deaf and Dumb Man, the Blind Man of Bethsaida, the Epileptic Boy. John's Gospel gives five, which, though edited, were originally Novellen, namely, the Marriage at Cana, the Nobleman's Son, the Lame Man at the Pool, the Man Born Blind, the Raising of Lazarus. Luke gives one, but it has been edited by him, namely, the Widow's Son at Nain.

These Tales have a definite form, for there is a

common technique in the descriptions. The history of the illness is first described, then follows the account of the cure, and lastly the result of the cure. Any remarks of a pragmatic character, such as the injunctions to secrecy, found in some of the Marcan stories, are the work of the evangelist. The Paradigms and Novellen were originally separate and independent units but were put into a framework by Mark under the influence of his doctrinal aim.

A third group consists of the Sayings, which served the purpose of catechetical teaching. They are of general application. There was an original and early collection of these sayings from Jewish and Hellenistic sources.

A fourth group is composed of Legends. A Legend is " a narrative written in an edifying style and telling of extraordinary things about a holy man or a holy place." In short it is a " religious narrative of a saintly man." The term does not mean that the story is unhistorical. " It does not exclude historical traits, but only says that the main interest of the narrative lies elsewhere than in the historicity; it is directed to the religiousness and sanctity of the hero." (*Fresh Approach to the New Testament*, p. 43.)

Legends were meant to meet a double need—to give some knowledge of the holy men and women who were associated with Jesus, their virtues and their fate, and to know Jesus Himself in this way. The Birth and Infancy Stories are amongst the Legends. " The Infancy story is a collection of legends of varied content and at different levels of historical significance."

These Legends show at what points primitive
Christian literature developed " in the direction of
the world." This secularization occurs very little
in the Gospels and is a sign that the tradition of
Jesus was at first barred to worldly influences but
was only so influenced when Christianity itself
entered further into " the world."

Lastly there are the Mythen. These Myths
describe " a many-sided interaction between mythological but not human persons." There are
three of them, the Baptism, the Temptation, the
Transfiguration.

As for the Passion Narrative, this was the only
continuous narrative in existence in the earliest
period. The earliest Christians read a gospel of
the Passion into the Old Testament and thus held
that certain details, such as the mocking and the
parting of the garments, were attested by being
in the Old Testament. In this way they gained
assurance that God had so willed it. Mark has
left a trace of an older Passion story in Chapter xiv,
verse 2, for the verse means that Jesus was put
to death at latest on the day before the Feast.

Dibelius thinks that at first anonymous people
made small collections, not to write books but to
pass on tradition. Even the earliest evangelists
did nothing else. " Thus the tradition of Jesus
only gradually became literature, and this took place
not on account of the literary ability of any author
but by virtue of the significance of its content."
(*Fresh Approach to the New Testament*, p. 53.)

Bultmann finds that there were problems which
Schmidt had not faced. Were the traditional
sections edited by the evangelists? Was the tradi-

tion historical? He himself asks whether literary forms may not be found in the Synoptic gospels conforming to the laws of style in all primitive literature such as the psalms, narratives, fables, prayers, etc., of the Old Testament?

He disagrees with the constructive method of Dibelius for he fails to see that the primary aim of the Churches was preaching or that the material was determined by the needs of such preaching. His own view is that much may be assigned to the controversies in the early Church.

Bultmann's grouping of the Gospel material is as follows. Apothegms, which may be controversial or biographical. This is practically the group called Paradigms by Dibelius. Then there are the Sayings which he subdivides into five groups, Wisdom Words, " I " Words, Prophetic and Apocalyptic Words, Law Words and Community Rules, and Parables. Only about forty of these sayings are trustworthy. The third group is that of Miracle-Stories which contain no history. The fourth group consists of Legends which are of no value.

Beginning with the Miracle Stories and Apothegms, Bultmann argues that all but a very few such as the Tribute Money and the Anointing are unhistorical. These stories were created by the Christian community, where they first arose, and can be explained either by the Christian situation or by the experiences of Christians. Yet the Apothegms may contain many historical sayings of Jesus.

He therefore proceeds to examine the sayings of Jesus to see what evidences they give of authenticity. He finds that some of the sayings are interpretations of the evangelists, others are due to the prophets of the early Church and were attributed to Jesus or first arose in the Christian community.

Thus, by a process of exclusion, he comes to the following conclusion. " The investigation of the sayings of Jesus leads to a considerable uncertainty, but it does not end in complete scepticism.   By no means are we at the mercy of those who doubt or deny that Jesus ever lived. . . . The *character* of Jesus, the vivid picture of his personality and his life, cannot now be clearly made out; but what is more important, the context of his message is or will be ever more clearly recognizable " (p. 61).

We get no historical account of the life of Christ. Even the Passion Story is overgrown with Legends. The final motive which produced the Gospels is not historical interest in Jesus but cultic, that is the needs of common worship.   The Passion Narrative was early in existence but even in Mark was given its form in the interests of the cultus or for edificatory and apologetic purposes.   The Resurrection narrative is due mainly to Christian imagination.

.   .   .   .   .   .

We shall discuss and examine at great length the standpoint and views of Schmidt, Dibelius and Bultmann in our later chapters.   We close this chapter with a few quotations from an English supporter of Form Criticism who is an ardent supporter of Wrede and Dibelius.   Though he warns us against the scepticism of Bultmann he re-echoes the conclusions to which the sceptical Bultmann was led.

R. H. LIGHTFOOT in his Bampton Lectures on *History and Interpretation in the Gospels*, admits that the task of Form Criticism " is bound to be more speculative than the literary comparison of the three Synoptic gospels and the results reached will be less susceptible of proof " (p. 33).   He warns us that Bultmann " is apt to set forth conclusions which will seem to many needlessly negative in character " (p. 43, note) but to our surprise, in spite of these warnings, he ends his lectures with words which are very like those of Bultmann. " It seems, then, that the form of the earthly no less than of the heavenly Christ is for the most part hidden from us. For all the inestimable value of the gospels, they yield us little more than a whisper of his voice; we trace in them but the outskirts of his ways " (p. 225).

No student of Form Criticism can neglect Lightfoot's warnings, nor that of Fascher, a German scholar, who has written a history of Form Criticism.[1] Fascher forcibly and wisely points out that " form alone permits no historical value judgments," that " Form Criticism is not in itself a historical tool," and that Form Critics might have found the life situation not in the community but in Jesus Himself.

[1] *The Form-Historical Method.*

Chapter II

THE ASSUMPTIONS OF FORM CRITICISM

Form Criticism is a study of probabilities. It is a speculative method of research. In Literary Criticism, on the other hand, the actual texts of the Gospels are the basis of work and by studying these documents certain conclusions as to sources can be drawn with some confidence, such as the priority of Mark and the existence of a source of sayings. Form Critics however are like explorers in unknown regions who must needs make a series of assumptions for their quest, and test every stage of their progress. Yet Form Criticism must lead somewhere even if it were only to the hinterland of the unknown. It is these hypotheses made by one or more of the Form Critics which must be discussed before the actual "forms" of the Gospel narratives and sayings are examined.

ASSUMPTION ONE. BEFORE THE GOSPELS WERE WRITTEN THERE WAS A PERIOD OF ORAL TRADITION

This can be confidently admitted, but opinion will vary on the extent of the formative period. Luke, in his preface to the Gospel, asserts that, before he wrote his record, others had been at pains in drawing up narratives of the facts of our Lord's ministry. Now Form Critics allow that Passion Narratives were written at an early period. Dibelius allows that " at an early date, viz. already in the time of Paul, words of Jesus had been collected for hortatory purposes " and that the source Q " gives a rough idea of such a collection " (pp. 242 ff.). Thus it is allowed by some Form Critics that not only collections of sayings but also a narrative of a special character were written quite early in the Christian era. Let us accept the chronology of the New Testament which Dibelius gives. Jesus was crucified about A.D. 30, Paul was converted within the period A.D. 32–35, and the Apostolic Council was held in A.D. 49–50. Now according to 1 Cor. xi and xv, certain traditions were received by the Apostle. " Thus as early as the fourth decade there were already in existence texts in Greek about events from the life of Jesus." About that time, Paul also received collections of sayings referred to in 1 Cor. vii and ix. " Hence, we may assert that the weighty elements of the tradition had become fixed in the first twenty years after Jesus' death . . . while eyewitnesses still lived, and when the events were only about a generation old." By the weighty elements Dibelius, it may be inferred from his book, means the Paradigms (p. 27 *supra*), the Passion Narrative, the list of Resurrection appearances in 1 Cor. xv, and a collection of sayings.

Elsewhere, I have suggested, on other grounds (Redlich p. 66), that there is reason for believing that Q was written about A.D. 50, about " twenty years after Jesus' death," and I am glad to have the corroboration of Dibelius. Further, if we admit that Luke had made a record of stories of our Lord during his stay at Caesarea, and had later utilized this record, L, in writing the Gospel as we have it, we begin to see that the middle of the first century in the Christian era is a critical date in Form Criticism. This means, in our view, that the formative period is not the interval of time between our Lord's death and the production of Mark, somewhere in the sixth or seventh decade, but between our Lord's death and the Apostolic Council, not two generations but scarcely one generation. The formative period was relatively a short one, and written records were made during the lifetime of the Apostles.

Not all Form Critics admit the presence of eye-witnesses of our Lord's ministry, death and resurrection. If they are right, says Vincent Taylor, " the disciples must have been translated to heaven immediately after the resurrection " (p. 41).

It will not follow that every detail of every narrative of our Lord's life can be guaranteed to be historically true because eye witnesses were alive when the first records were made. We must allow for personal errors, want of powers of scientific observation, the Eastern outlook and modes of thought, misunderstandings and such like. Our claim is that there is *prima-facie* ground for assuming the substantial accuracy of the Gospel narrative.

It is a reasonable charge against Form Critics that they do not allow or admit some of the contributions of Literary Criticism. The evidence for the existence of L is a case in point, and there is some ground for accepting the statement that this written record was made about twenty years after our Lord's death.

The first assumption of Form Criticism therefore requires some definition and qualification.

ASSUMPTION TWO.   DURING THE ORAL PERIOD, THE
   NARRATIVES AND SAYINGS, WITH THE EXCEPTION OF
   THE PASSION NARRATIVE, CIRCULATED MAINLY AS
   SINGLE AND SELF-CONTAINED DETACHED UNITS,
   EACH COMPLETE IN ITSELF.

This assumption is based on another, namely the
theory that the contexts are of no value.   It is
Schmidt's well-known argument that Mark is of
no biographical or chronological or geographical
interest.   The editor's insertion must be removed,
and when this has been done, the Form Critics hope
to get back to the stories as they were current in the
oral period.   The units have no context and no
historical setting.   We shall deal with this theory
later.   (See Assumption Five.)

The meaning of the second assumption is that,
in the main, (a) Each of the narrative units was a
little separate story.   For example, the Tribute
Money, the Withered Hand, Blessing the Children,
etc., circulated separately and independently. (b)
The sayings of our Lord similarly circulated in
isolation or in small collections.

The assumption can be accepted but not wholly.
Albertz, one of the Form Critical school, who
specialized in the study of the controversial arguments
of the synoptic gospels, admitted that a narrative
collection existed in Mark ii, 1–iii, 6, and that
xi, 15–xii, 40, which is composed of narrative and
parable, was a complete unit.   Lightfoot admits
the possibility that " certain groups of stories were
already in existence, perhaps in a written form,
before St. Mark embodied them in his fuller work "
(p. 37, note).

First then as to the narratives.   It is claimed by

Dibelius (p. 307) that over fifty self-contained para-
graphs may be found in Mark, e.g. the Cleansing of
the Leper (i, 40–45), the Choice of the Twelve (iii,
13–19), the Death of John the Baptist (vi, 14–29),
the Syro-Phoenician Woman (vii, 24–30), the
Widow's Mite (xii, 41–44), the Last Supper (xiv,
22–25), the Empty Tomb (xvi, 1–8).

But there are sections in the Gospel which bear
evidence in themselves that they each formed a
complete series before they reached the evangelist.
The first section which is a complete unit of stories
is that which covers i, 21–39. It is intrinsically
impossible to discard the editorial matter or to
refuse to see in this section the personal reminiscences of an eyewitness, who was undoubtedly
Simon Peter. The connecting links make a complete story of a day's work. Let us gather the
connecting links together.

" And they go into Capernaum; and straightway
on the sabbath day he (Jesus) entered into a synagogue and taught." The effect of the teaching is
followed by the cure of a man with an unclean spirit.

" And straightway, when they were come out of
the synagogue, they came into the house of Simon
and Andrew, with James and John." The cure of
Simon's wife's mother follows.

" And at even, when the sun did set, they brought
unto him all that were sick." The healings follow.

" And in the morning, a great while before day,
he rose up and went out, and departed into a desert
place, and there prayed."

The notes of time are too definite to be artificial
or literary. They read like a consecutive narrative,
honestly reported and repeated. The narrator

gives the impression of having been there when the things happened.

The second group is the series of conflict stories (ii, 1–iii, 6) in which the opposition to Jesus grows more intense as we proceed, and ends up with the statement, " And the Pharisees went out, and straightway with the Herodians took counsel against him, how they might destroy him." Now, we do not hear of the Herodians again till xii, 13, and here too they are united with the Pharisees. This second mention of Herod's party-men is followed by two conflict stories, the Tribute Money and the Resurrection (xii, 13–27). It has been frequently noted that the opposition stories come too early in the Marcan narrative, and that the group of stories is artificially arranged. It is quite possible, therefore, that ii, 1—iii, 6, which ends with a plot to kill Jesus may with xii, 13–27, have formed an introduction to a Passion Narrative; that there was a complete block of seven independent narratives which was current as a unit in the early days and reached Mark in that form, but that it was divided by him into two sections.

The section iv, 35—v, 43, is in the nature of an itinerary. Dibelius says that probably the whole cycle arose before Mark. " Here it is topography which holds the first stories together, for the healing of the demoniac had to take place in Gentile country, and hence there must be a sea-crossing " (p. 219). Schmidt too thinks it possible that this block reached Mark as a complete unit.

Then we come to two sections, each of which contains a story of the feeding of a multitude. It has long been suspected, and by some scholars accepted as possible, that vi, 30—vii, 37 and viii, 1–26, are parallel accounts of the same series of events and that two accounts were in circulation, which though doublets, were accepted by Mark. Easton has called attention to the remarkable chain of doublets in each cycle—a story of the feeding of the multitude, a journey across the lake, a controversy, departure from Galilee, a saying about bread and a healing. " As we cannot believe that Mark was consciously responsible for this long chain of doublets, we must suppose that the two series were circulated separately and that the evangelist combined them " (p. 72).

Lastly, we have Albertz's section xi, 15—xii, 40, describing the entry into Jerusalem, followed by the events of the Monday and Tuesday. Jesus enters Jerusalem (xi, 1–10), goes into the Temple (xi, 11), spends the night in Bethany (xi, 11 f.) returns to the city on the Monday, casts out the dealers there (xi, 15–18) and in the evening goes out of the city (xi, 19). Next morning Jesus comes again to Jerusalem (xi, 20, 27). We have here a consecutive chain of events, very similar to the day in our Lord's life in Capernaum, with indications of place and time.

Hence we conclude that Mark found in tradition a number of separate *pericopae*, as well as a number of blocks of narratives connected together either by a common topical interest or by an orderly succession in time or in the form of an itinerary. Some of these incidents may have previously existed separately but that does not disprove our contention that the early Church was interested in matters of time and place and was not devoid of the desire to know something of what Jesus did, where He happened to be, and when He performed certain miracles or uttered His sayings. This interest is evident in Luke and Matthew. For example, Luke connects the question of fasting with the eating with publicans and sinners, which are detached units in Mark, by the words " And the Pharisees and their scribes murmured against his disciples " (Luke v, 29–35, Mark ii, 15–20). Matthew similarly connects the Blessing of Children with what precedes and follows (Matthew ix, 13, 15, 16).

We must next consider the sayings. Here we come across blocks of sayings so remarkably arranged that we are justified in concluding that some of them at least can be attributed to our Lord, who, in so arranging them, was following the usual procedure of Rabbis.

There are three groups of sayings which are artificial in character and arranged that they might be easily learnt and remembered. (a) Mark iv, 21–25, with its catchwords " lamp " and " light " on the one hand, and " measure," " more given " and " taken away." The catchwords suggest two separate groups of two verses each. (b) Mark viii, 34—ix, 1, with constant references to life, the " saving his life " and " losing his life." (c) Mark ix, 41–50, consisting of two groups, the first dealing with the idea of stumbling, and passing on, from causing the little ones to stumble, to " If thy hand. . . . If thy foot. . . . If thine eye cause thee to stumble "; the second group dealing with references to salt. The first group is probably a saying of Christ for its parallelism is too pronounced to be artificial, the second may be Marcan.

It is when we turn to Matthew and Luke that we
encounter a remarkable series of blocks which
suggest Rabbinical methods of teaching and point
to the literary skill of a genius.   Let us take our
Lord's teaching on Providence (Matthew vi, 25–32).
The theme is given in v. 25.

> Be not anxious for your life,
>> What ye shall eat,
>> Or what ye shall drink;
> Nor yet for your body,
>> What ye shall put on.
> Is not the life more than the food,
>> And the body than the raiment?

Then in keeping with the sequence of food and
clothing, we get Christ's words on food first (vv.
26–27) beginning with:

> Behold, the birds of the heaven,

and then going on to clothing (vv. 28–30).

> Why are ye anxious concerning raiment?

The poem concludes (v. 31) first with words in
keeping with the introductory theme,

> Be not therefore anxious,
> Saying, What shall we eat?
> Or, What shall we drink?
> Or, Wherewithal shall we be clothed?

And this leads on to a message, giving further
lessons on Providence.

Another primitive block may be observed in
Matthew v, 17–48 with which Taylor has dealt at
some length (p. 97).   The keynote is given in the
opening words, " Think not that I came to destroy
the law or the prophets " and these are soon followed
by six sections which open with the phrase " Ye have

heard that it was said to them of old time " . . . and later continues " but I say unto you." Taylor refers to Albertz who, in studying the whole block, says that, when the Q portions are removed, the structural form becomes evident, for what is left are passages with a genuine antithetical form. Albertz can see no reason why the grouping should not have been the work of Jesus. To this primitive and original complex, Matthew added sayings from Q and other matter. The primitive unit, according to Albertz, is verses 17, 21–22a, 27f, 33–34a, and 37, and will read as follows :

17 Think not that I came to destroy the law or the
        prophets :
    I came not to destroy, but to fulfil.

21 Ye have heard that it was said of them of old time,
        Thou shalt not kill ;
    And whosoever shall kill
        Shall be in danger of the judgment :

22 But I say unto you,
        Every one who is angry with his brother
        Shall be in danger of the judgment ;

27 Ye have heard that it was said
        Thou shalt not commit adultery.

28 But I say unto you,
        Every one that looketh on a woman to lust after her
        Hath committed adultery with her already in his
            heart.

33 Ye have heard that it was said to them of old time
        Thou shalt not forswear thyself,
        But shalt perform unto the Lord thine oaths.

34 But I say unto you,
        Swear not at all.

37   But let your speech be, yea, yea; Nay, nay;
      And whatsoever is more than these is of the evil one.

Easton calls attention to a block in Luke vi, 27–38. He points out that in vv. 27–30 four clauses are balanced by four others and are followed by a summary in v. 31 and similarly throughout the block, a summary being also found in v. 35, and the theme of v. 36 being elaborated in vv. 37–38a. We give the first five verses only for the present:

27   Love your enemies,
      Do good to them that hate you.

28   Bless them that curse you,
      · Pray for them that despitefully use you.

29   To him that smiteth thee on the one cheek, offer also
      the other;
      And from him that taketh thy cloke withhold not thy
      coat also.

30   Give to every one that asketh thee;
      And of him that taketh away thy goods ask them not
      again.

31   And as ye would that men should do to you,
      Do ye also to them likewise.

Easton pertinently reminds us that, as a Rabbi, Jesus would require His disciples to memorize His teaching. He had only a short time in which to impress His teaching, whereas an ordinary Rabbi had a whole lifetime. " We have every reason to believe that the first tradition of the sayings-groups and the parables arose in Jesus' lifetime and under His personal direction " (*Christ in the Gospels*, p. 41).

Regularity of structure may be seen in Christ's words on almsgiving, prayer and fasting (Matthew vi), and in Luke xi, 42–52, where three woes on the

Pharisees are paralleled by three woes on the lawyers. So also Luke vi, 32–35, is a stanza group with a concluding summary in which the second and third lines of the first three verses should be noticed, as also the summary with " love " and " do good " and " lend," which are the keywords of the three preceding verses.

32 If ye love them that love you,
         What thank have ye?
     For even sinners love those that love them.

33 If ye do good to them that do good to you,
         What thank have ye?
     For even sinners do the same.

34 If ye lend to them of whom ye hope to receive,
         What thank have ye?
     Even sinners lend to sinners to receive again as much.

35 But love your enemies, and do good, and lend,
         Never despairing;
     And your reward shall be great,
     And ye shall be sons of the Most High.

We may therefore claim that there are blocks of sayings in the Gospels which may be traced to Jesus Himself. His teaching had to be intensive, and yet had to be remembered, and there is evidence to show that His skill and His genius was such that He succeeded in His aim and purpose.

We can now turn to the contribution of the late C. F. Burney in *The Poetry of our Lord*. He is at one with Easton in attributing much of the sayings to our Lord. He contends that considerable portions of our Lord's sayings are cast in the form of Hebrew poetry, and therefore is evident proof of authenticity. Illustrations of poetical form can be perceived even in an English translation, though naturally much clearer if the Greek text were put into Aramaic. We take some examples.

Synonymous Parallelism. A couplet in which the two lines correspond in idea, the second line re-echoing the first in different terms. For example:

> Be not anxious for your life, what ye shall eat,
> Neither for your body, what ye shall put on:
> Is not the life more than meat?
> And the body than raiment?
>
> Is it lawful on the sabbath to do good or to do harm?
> To save a life or to kill.
>
> There is nothing hid that shall not be made manifest,
> Nor secret that shall not come to light.

Antithetical Parallelism. Here the parallelism is carried out by contrast between the terms of the second line and those of the first. For example:

> He that findeth his life shall lose it;
> And he that loseth his life for My sake shall find it.
>
> The Sabbath was made for man,
> And not man for the sabbath.
>
> Every good tree bringeth forth good fruit
> But the corrupt tree bringeth forth evil fruit.

This form of parallelism, says Burney, is " widespread " in our Lord's teaching, and is found in all the Gospels. " This is conclusive evidence that our Lord did so frame His teaching." Maxims in this form could easily be remembered. " In this and in similar forms of antithesis we may surely believe that we possess our Lord's *ipsissima verba* more nearly than in any sentence otherwise expressed."

Synthetic or Constructive Parallelism. The parallelism here is not in thought but in form only. The thought of the second line supplements and com-

pletes that of the first.   The sense flows on con-
tinuously.

> They make broad their phylacteries
> And enlarge their fringes.

> And love the chief place at the feasts
> And the chief seats in the synagogues.

> And the salutations in the market places,
> And to be called of men, Rabbi.

> But be not ye called Rabbi
> For one is your teacher,
> And all ye are brethren.

> And call no man your father on earth;
> For One is your Father, the heavenly.

> Neither be ye called masters;
> For One is your Master, even Christ.

Burney argues that the presence of formal
characteristics of Hebrew poetry is a strong argument for substantial authenticity.   This is more
reasonable than that the various writers of our
Lord's teaching should have acted independently
and produced results essentially identical in form.

Rhythm.   The correspondence between member
and member in couplets is noticeable.   An example
from synonymous parallelism is :

> Give not | the holy thing | to the dogs,
> And cast not | your pearls | before swine.

So also in antithetical parallelism :

> He that is faithful | in little, | is faithful | in much;
> And he that is dishonest| in little, | is dishonest | in much.

Also in quatrains in which parallelism is found not
between successive lines, but between alternate
lines :

If ye forgive | to men | their trespasses,
Your Father | in heaven | shall forgive you;

But if ye forgive not | to men | their trespasses,
Neither shall your Father | forgive | your trespasses.

" The Synoptic evidence suggests that our Lord varied the form in which He conveyed His teaching to His disciples."

Thus we may reasonably infer that this familiar rhythm was well remembered, and is a record of words in the form in which they were conveyed.

Burney's argument enables us to make an advance on that of Dibelius. The German scholar argued that written collections of sayings existed before A.D. 50. We may go further and say that collections were made and remembered very soon after our Lord's death, when memories were fresh and vivid. The sayings taught in easily remembered poetical forms would be written down and used for catechetical purposes in the early Church in order that instruction should be given to those converts who joined the body known as " Those of the Way "—a significant designation in connection with the new teaching which had to replace the old.

Thus the assumption that during the oral period the narratives and sayings circulated in little separate units requires qualification. It is quite possible, as the evidence of the Gospels shows, that often narratives were grouped together for mnemonic purposes, through a living interest in details of our Lord's life, and through association with places and districts. On the other hand, many a story circulated independently and it is impossible to assign them to a particular period of the ministry. As for the sayings, these too circulated in collections or in isolation, and the evidence for their authenticity is strong and reasonable. Bultmann's verdict that only about forty of them are genuine is manifestly absurd. It is possible that collections of sayings were put into writing within ten years of our Lord's death, if the tradition, which Paul states that he received, was given him on his first visit to Jerusalem when he stayed with Peter and was in the company of James, the Lord's brother, for some days (Gal. i, 18 f.) There could only have been one topic in that home—Jesus, who went about doing good and taught the way of salvation.

We may here call attention to the words " according to the scriptures," which were used by St. Paul. " For I delivered unto you first of all that which also I received, how that Christ died for our sins according to the scriptures; and that he was buried; and that he hath been raised on the third day according to the scriptures " (1 Cor. xv, 3 f.). Bussmann is of opinion that the common explanation that reference was made by Paul to the Old Testament is erroneous, for whenever the Apostle refers to the Old Testament he uses the singular " the scripture," except in three cases which are not really exceptions to this rule (Rom. i, 2; xv, 4; xvi, 26). Bussmann holds therefore that the Apostle is appealing to " accounts of the Passion Story existing in the community, perhaps even to one or some of the attempts at Gospel-writings mentioned by Luke." Vincent Taylor to whom I owe this reference (p. 49) says that in default of Bussmann's explanation, it will be necessary to interpret the passage in Corinthians as a reference to the Old

D

Testament, which is unsatisfactory, or to a collection
of Testimonies from the Scriptures.

ASSUMPTION THREE. THE MATERIAL IN THE GOSPELS CAN BE CLASSIFIED ACCORDING TO THEIR FORM

The natural division of the subject matter of the
Gospels is into narratives and sayings. But Form
Critics have done good service by observing that
many of the narratives, even some hitherto called
miracles, were valued in the early Church not as
stories but for the sayings in them, and that the
interest in them was a pronouncement of Jesus.

We shall be discussing the various groups in
succeeding chapters, and our aim here is simply an
examination of the hypothesis. Can the material
be classified according to form? In other words,
is form present in all the material? Let us consider
the main divisions of the material.

1. *Sayings, including parables.* Bultmann who
made a thorough study of the sayings divided them
into five groups, Wisdom words or Logia, " I "
words, i.e., sayings in the first person singular,
Prophetic and Apocalyptic words, Law words and
Community Rules, Parables. But these classifications show immediately that the basis of division is
not one of form but of contents. The limitations of
Form Criticism are therefore evident for the
categories are characteristic of the content of the
Gospel and not formal. Easton has a pertinent
remark to make on this division of sayings. " What
form difference is there between the ' logion '—
Whosoever exalteth himself shall be humbled "—
the ' apocalyptic word '—Whosoever shall be

ashamed of me, the Son of man shall be ashamed of him—and the ' church rule '—Whosoever putteth away his wife and marrieth another committeth adultery?" (p. 74).

The only category which shows any form is that of the Parables. No distinctions which are based on subject matter are distinctions of form. Thus all the attempts made to classify the sayings are of no use in Form Criticism. And, in fact, there is no evidence that the evangelists were interested in classifying sayings to the extent that Bultmann suggests. Any classification that can be traced is that of poetical form or subject matter; oral tradition cared not for such things as form or the history of form. The primitive Church was unconscious of forms.

2. *Apothegm-Stories*. These are narratives in which the main interest is concentrated on a saying or pronouncement of Jesus, which is the kernel of the story. No attempt is made to describe the situation and only so much is stated as will make the saying intelligible.

The terminology given to this type of material varies. Dibelius calls them Paradigms, because he thinks that they were used as models or illustrations in preaching. The term Paradigm is therefore no indication of form but of the function which the narrative is thought to fulfil. Further, by associating the term with a special life-situation, it excludes the possibility of others. Bultmann calls these stories Apothegms, because they show close similarity with sayings so called in Greek literature. But this is to overlook the narrative element which gives life and meaning to the saying. Fascher uses the term

Dialogues, but this is too exclusive and limits the number of this type of narrative. Taylor suggests Pronouncement-Stories which is apt and covers the type. If I suggest Apothegm-Stories, it is because the word Apothegm is distinctive in meaning, and by joining the word " stories " to it, the failure in overlooking the narrative element is safe-guarded. The type stands midway between a narrative and an independent saying, and by placing the term Apothegm before " stories," the importance of the saying in a narrative framework is emphasized.

There is no unanimity with regard to the number of this class. Much depends on the extent of the formal characteristics. For example, should such a narrative mention names? Bultmann says that the presence of personal names is a sign that the narratives are unhistorical. The justification for this conclusion is not clear. Dibelius, though he will not allow that the narratives are unhistorical, thinks that the names were a later insertion. He thinks also that where names are inseparably connected with persons, such as Martha and Mary, the incident must not be classed amongst his Paradigms. The decision regarding the number of Apothegm-Stories is therefore not a simple process.

3. *Miracle-Stories or Wonder-Stories.* These have a simple form which is universal, and not confined to the Gospels. The three formal characteristics of the healing stories are, the description of the ailment, the cure with a possible reference to the means used, and the effect of the cure. In them, the interest is directed to the narrative for its own sake, there is more detail than in the Apothegm-Stories, and more vividness in description; also

secular, as distinct from religious, elements are present. The stories were valued not for any saying which might be recorded in the course of the narrative but because Jesus was there set forth as a thaumaturge.

The terminology is open to criticism in two directions. The stories have a form, but to call them Miracle-Stories is to designate not their form but their contents. Also, in describing the stories as those of Jesus as a miracle worker, there is no indication of the faith of those who were recipients of our Lord's works of healing and power. No other term however can be suggested, except " Miracles which possess form."

Dibelius uses the term Novellen because they were produced by a body of story-tellers. He has been influenced therefore by his constructive method. We may justifiably question the existence of a particular body of story-tellers in the Church— there is no trace of them in the New Testament— and we may ask why Peter himself might not have been one of the story tellers, as indeed the unnamed young man of Mark xiv, 51 is admitted to have been.

4. *Stories, Legends and Myths*. Outside the Apothegm-Stories and Miracle-Stories, which contain forms, are to be found many narratives without any distinctive form. These have been variously classified according to their contents or according to the subjective judgment of each Form Critic. For example we read of:

Stories of Jesus, of which there are about forty, apart from the Birth, Passion and Resurrection of Jesus.

Legends which are to some extent but not altogether

stories of others than Jesus; Bultmann considers them valueless as history.

Myths which describe actions of divine beings.

The terms Legend and Myth are objectionable to English students for they are judgments of the historic value of the narratives and are of a disparaging character. They also imply that the events included in them serve no soteriological purpose. If Form Criticism deals with forms and attempts to classify forms and to trace the history of forms and to discover the processes of their growth, their method is regular. But to use terms which pass an initial judgment on the historical value of stories and to classify them not according to form but according to the critic's own view of their veracity, is very irregular and unjustifiable. Form Criticism then becomes a judgment of truth or falsity, and not a scientific method of research.

R. H. Lightfoot has said some wise words on this matter of classification and I do not hesitate in quoting them at length. " Naturally enough, in the excitement of a comparatively recent discovery, our new guides tend to see in it a key which may be used to unlock every door, and they are prepared to classify all the different sections in these chapters (Mark i–xiii) under an appropriate type or heading, according to the nature of their content. It is likely that the material will prove too complex and difficult for such rigorous treatment; and for the present at any rate it will suffice to draw attention to the two main kinds of stories about Jesus which are found in our earliest gospel. In the first of these, a saying of his is the climax or at least the leading feature of the story; in the second, the emphasis is on an act of power done by him.   It seems at least possible that the new study has here achieved a valuable and lasting result, and that it has succeeded in distinguishing and classifying two types of story, both of which are prominent in St. Mark " (p. 43).

We conclude therefore that the assumption that the material can be classified according to their form is only true in part and in a very restricted manner.   The only classification that can be made is that (*a*) as regards the sayings, there is a group with form, if we omit poetical form, namely the Parables, and (*b*) the narrative portions contain two groups which possess form, namely Apothegm-Stories and Miracle-Stories.   The greater part of the material is " form "-less.

ASSUMPTION FOUR.   THE VITAL FACTORS WHICH GAVE RISE TO AND PRESERVED THESE FORMS ARE TO BE FOUND IN THE PRACTICAL INTERESTS OF THE CHRISTIAN COMMUNITY

The principle underlying this hypothesis is that the practical needs of the early Church, particularly in spreading abroad the message of salvation through Christ, gave rise to the forms of the tradition, which by constant repetition during the oral period became fixed in characteristics.

We may take the views of Dibelius on Paradigms as an illustration.   He associates these formal narratives with the earliest preaching of missionaries, and, in the course of his argument, lays down the thesis that they must possess universal application since a special application in a concrete case was of no use in preaching.   When, for instance, Jesus said " Behold my mother and my brethren," Jesus was

speaking with the immediate circle in view.   Those
who were round Him at the time were His " mother
and brethren."   This was a concrete case.   But as
the narrative stood it was of no practical use as an
appeal in preaching.   It was necessary to add a
universal application which would bring in would-be
converts.   Hence a preacher added the words
" Whosoever shall do the will of God, the same is
my brother, and sister, and mother."   Thus, if we
remove the universal application, we get the original
form of the narrative and the pre-paradigm stage of
the saying.   Similarly, all elements in a Paradigm
which are not necessary for the lesson which Jesus
intended to teach can be removed.   The Paradigm
must have a conventional form to give the hearers a
vivid picture of Jesus ; this form was created by
eliminating needless additions and concentrating
on the saying.   Hence a Paradigm is not wholly a
record of objective fact, but the true record can be
discovered.

Dibelius held that Paradigms were used as models
or illustrations in Christian preaching, that sayings
were collected for exhortation, and that Miracle-
Stories were the creation of a body of story-tellers
in the Church and would also serve as guides for
Christian healers.   Bultmann was of opinion that
the narrative material for the most part was used for
cultic purposes, such as worship or edification, as
well as for polemical or apologetic ends.   As regards the sayings, the greater part of them originated
in Christian communities and were then attributed
to Jesus.

First, then, as to the sayings.   Our criticism is
that the life-situation might just as readily be found in

Jesus Himself, and that the community preserved the sayings because they were vital and authoritative pronouncements of Jesus. Paul gives definite evidence that this was the case, and he is careful to distinguish between the words of Jesus and his own dicta. " But to the rest say I, not the Lord." " Now concerning virgins I have no commandment of the Lord : but I give my judgment " (1 Cor. vii, 10, 13, 25). So also in Q, which is a collection of our Lord's sayings. There we find answers to questions which were the immediate concern of the early Christian Church at Antioch. Was a gentile Church in accordance with the views of Jesus? Was Antioch justified in separating from the Christian community? How was the Christian community to meet opposition and calumny? Was Christian baptism necessary or would John's baptism be sufficient? What did Jesus teach on all these matters as well as on missionary enterprise? What was His teaching on social questions and on morals? The whole contents of Q give our Lord's guidance on the varied needs of the Antiochene Church (Redlich, pp. 51–71).

Again, we know as a fact of experience, that a saying must come initially from an individual. A community cannot create a saying; only an individual can. A community can only transmit and preserve a saying. And when we survey the conditions of the early Church we find no personalities gifted with the power of creating original sayings such as we find in the Gospels. Even such a prolific writer like Paul was careful to underline the binding power of the dicta of Jesus. When we consider the scope and breadth and poetic skill of

the sayings, and realize that they form a corpus of
utterances, unrivalled in comparison with such books
as the Wisdom of Solomon or the Wisdom of the
Son of Sirach or the Proverbs, we must either conclude that they came from a single genius greater
than Solomon or that the Church contained many
Solomons or many prophets greater than the
prophets of old. The only solution is that the
sayings were the sayings of one personality. No
other explanation can meet the circumstances.

The Christian community would certainly have
utilized the sayings for the propagation of the Gospel
as well as for all the multiple interests of the Church.
Any evaluation of the vital factors will show us not
how the structural forms, if any there be, arose but
what part of the whole body of sayings was retained.
That the views and beliefs to some extent influenced
and modified the tradition cannot be denied, that
sayings circulated in more than one form is evidenced
in the gospels, but, in the main, the teaching of
Jesus was well and carefully preserved.

These statements of ours do not concern the forms
of the sayings. Except the parables, the sayings
have no formal characteristics. But they are our
answer, first, to Bultmann's view that imagination
played a great part in the attribution of sayings of
the community to Jesus, and, secondly, our support
of the view that sayings were chiefly used for
edificatory purposes and that, for the greater part,
they are the sayings of Jesus.

" If we are to follow Wellhausen and Bultmann,"
wrote Easton, " we must hold that Jesus gave no
systematic teaching but was able, none the less, to
inspire his followers with the utmost moral and

literary discrimination; so much so that when they came to draw up rules for themselves they adopted only the basic contents of the Synoptists. That is, Wellhausen and Bultmann canonize the entire Palestinian Church!" (p. 118).

Then, as to the narratives. The proposition of Dibelius that the nearer a narrative is to a sermon the more reliable it is, means that his Paradigms are true but that the other stories are not all true historical records, that some of them are founded on historical events and others are unhistorical. This will need fuller examination (Chapters III, IV, VII). But is Dibelius justified in limiting the vital interests to " preaching," even though he uses it in a wide sense to include missionary preaching, sermons during worship, and catechetical teaching? Was there a body of story-tellers, of whose existence there is not a shred of evidence in the whole of the New Testament? Dibelius is justified in attempting a constructive method of study, when he investigates the vital interests of the primitive Church. Bultmann too is right in calling attention to the controversial and polemical questions which agitated the Church. But in any constructive method, all the interests of the Church should be surveyed, not only missions, apologetics, and teaching but questions relating to works of charity and mercy, home life, the treatment of children, the claims of the state, persecutions, neighbourliness, forgiveness of injuries, views of conflicting parties, deaths, marriages, enjoyment of nature and so on. The Acts, Q, and the Epistles bear witness to the multiplicity of interests which affected the life of the Church. However much the expected Parousia controlled the life and conduct of the early Christians we find them living a normal life, interested for example in supplying the needs of the poor (Acts iv, 34 ; vi, 1–6). Paul was insistent that the Corinthian Church should abound in the work of the Lord, " forasmuch as ye know that your labour is not vain in the Lord " (1 Cor. xv, 58). The stories would therefore illustrate and encourage Christians as well as would-be converts in giving teaching on all the practical interests of daily life.

The Church played its part in preserving the substantial accuracy of the facts. It may have set some of them, e.g. the Birth stories, in poetical form. Its narration of events may have been to some extent influenced by their beliefs as they were, for example, in the stories of demons, for the early Christians were ignorant of the psychology of insanity. It may have preserved stories of popular origin as in the death of John the Baptist. But in nearly every incident recorded the centre of interest was Jesus, who went about doing good. The Church preserved the tradition, but the Church was not more important than Jesus.

Form Criticism, however, by this assumption supports the view so strongly favoured by Canon Streeter that the Gospels were associated with the great centres of Christianity.

But some Form Critics in tracing the influence of the community mean to imply that much of the material, both narratives and sayings, were created by and in the communities. They were then attributed to Jesus. That is to say, the communities were bereft of apostles and eye-witnesses whose presence would check any unhistorical tendency.

They only created myths. The early primitive Church consisted of men and women who were under the influence of phantasy!

That interpretations of the community were given to some of the parables was the view of many scholars before Form Criticism began. For example, the Church was probably responsible for the explanations of the parables of the Sower and of the Tares, since the explanations turn simple parables into allegories. The interpretation of the Church may lie behind the statement that it was given in private (Mark iv, 10 ff, 34 f; vii, 18 ff; ix, 28 f).

But what about the attribution of the tenets of the early Church to Jesus? The extent of this influence may be evaluated in two ways. We can work forward from the teaching of Jesus and consider whether the problems He dealt with were only the interests of the early Church or we may work backward from the Apostolic age and consider whether its problems are dealt with in the gospels. Then we can ask ourselves the question, Does the Gospel tradition give us a faithful record of the problems of the ministry of our Lord or of the views and beliefs of the early Church?

Let us begin with the Gospels. We find that the term " Son of man " often stressed in the gospels is mentioned only once in the Acts (vii, 56), that a rough outline of the ministry is given in the preaching of Peter (Acts x, 36–43), that the miracles of Jesus are not used to prove His Messiahship which the community might have done for apologetic and polemical purposes, that though the questions of fasting, sabbath observance, sabbath healing, and Jewish laws of purity had only a historical interest for the early Church, yet Mark finds room for them.

On the other hand when we look backward from the Apostolic age, we find no references in Mark to prophecy and " tongues," no mention of the problem of circumcision, no view of Christ as omniscient or pre-existent, no reference to anointing with oil, no mention of the Church, only one reference to exorcism and that not by disciples (Mark ix, 38), only one to Christian baptism and that made by John the Baptist, if the words " with the Holy Ghost " are part of the true text, and only two directly referring to the extension of the Gospel to Gentiles (xiii, 10, xiv, 9). Easton who has a valuable chapter on this point entitled The Synoptic Perspective ends it with the words, " The primary historic value of the Synoptists is not for their own age but for the tradition of the teachings of Christ."

We conclude that the assumption should read, " The vital factors which preserved the tradition are to be found in the practical interests of the Christian community."

ASSUMPTION FIVE.   THE MATERIAL OF THE TRADITION
    HAS NO BIOGRAPHICAL OR CHRONOLOGICAL OR
    GEOGRAPHICAL VALUE

This means that Form Critics discard all contexts and sayings, refuse to allow for the evidence of eye-witnesses, attach very little significance to the evidence of the Acts and the Pauline epistles, and consider the evidence given by Papias of no intrinsic importance. In short, the contribution of Mark is held to be practically worthless and the Lucan prologue of no value.

Who were " the eye-witnesses and ministers of

the word?" Cadbury in a full critical study of the prologue to Luke's Gospel ends his commentary with the remark that the meaning of the prologue may be that " We Christians who have received the message " is opposed to the Christian " eye-witnesses and ministers of the word " who handed on the tradition. He is discussing the question of author-ship, which is not our concern, but goes on to say that the sense of the prologue may be, " Many have received it (the story) ; eye-witnesses and partici-pants have transmitted it ; I also, as one well-informed will narrate it."[1] Cadbury thus allows that eye-witnesses and participants transmitted the facts of the Gospel story, " the word." We may add that the Apostles were ministers of the word (Acts viii, 4). That " the word " included more than the doctrine is clear not only from the fact that Luke went on, after his prologue, to write both a record of our Lord's sayings and a story of His life, but also from the care taken in the election of a successor to Judas. Such a man had to possess the qualification of knowing the details of the ministry of Jesus " beginning from the baptism of John, unto the day that he was received up from us " (Acts i, 22).

The Kerygma. Form Critics because of their assumption that contexts and editorial redactions are of no historical value are inclined to limit the meaning of " the word." Dibelius asserts that Luke in his Prologue speaks " of those eye-witnesses and servants of the word who created tradition from which the composers of the Gospels drew their material " and later says, " The primitive Christians

[1] *The Beginnings of Christianity*, II, pp. 489–510.

did not relate the life of Jesus, but proclaimed the
salvation which had come about in Jesus. What
they narrated was secondary to this proclamation,
was intended to confirm it and to found it " (p. 15).
The " word " to Dibelius was the message of salvation, the primary part of which was not the narration
of the facts of our Lord's life.

It is therefore necessary that we should consider (1)
the evidence of the Acts and of the Epistles on the
contents of the preaching of the Apostles, (2) the
internal evidence of Mark on the presence of eye-
witnesses, (3) the external evidence of Papias, and
(4) the value of the chronology of Mark.

(1) *The Apostolic preaching*. Dibelius limits the
Kerygma to the opening theme of the preaching,
which was contained in a few short sentences at the
beginning (Acts ii, 22–24 ; viii, 13–21 ; x, 37–42 ;
xiii, 23–31). This is not justified, for the *Kerygma*
is a proclamation of the good news, as we shall see
presently, and is equivalent to the opening Marcan
phrase " The beginning of the gospel of Jesus
Christ."[1]

The evidence of the Epistles is conclusive on this
matter. The Epistles " presuppose the Preaching
(i.e. the *Kerygma*). They expound and defend the
implications of the Gospel rather than proclaim it."
The contents and main headings of the Preaching
may be gathered from references in the Epistles.

Galatians iii, 1. " Jesus Christ was openly set forth
crucified," before the eyes of the foolish Galatians.

1 Corinthians i, 23. " We preach Christ crucified, unto
Jews a stumbling block, and unto Gentiles foolishness."

[1] My indebtedness to Dodd's *The Apostolic Preaching* for this section
is great.

ii, 2, " I determined not to know anything among you, save Jesus Christ, and him crucified." xv, 1–11, " Now I make known unto you, brethren, the gospel which I preached unto you, which also ye received, wherein also ye stand, by which also ye are saved; I make known, I say, in what words I preached unto you, if ye hold it fast, except ye believed in vain. For I delivered unto you first of all that which also I received, how that Christ died for our sins according to the scriptures; and that he was buried; and that he hath been raised on the third day according to the scriptures; and that he appeared to Cephas; then to the twelve . . . Whether then it be I or they, so we preach, and so ye believed."

Paul clearly says the gospel he preached included the death and resurrection of Jesus. His preaching was what he received, and was identical with the preaching of the Apostles. The doctrinal significance of the preaching does not come within our inquiry.

Romans x, 8–9. " The word of faith, which we preach; because if thou shalt confess with thy mouth Jesus as Lord, and shalt believe in thy heart that God raised him from the dead, thou shalt be saved."

xiv, 9–10. " For to this end, Christ died, and lived again, that he might be Lord of both the dead and the living . . . for we shall all stand before the judgment-seat of God."

Here the proclamation of the resurrection is associated with the thought of Jesus as Lord. Judgment, we note, is part of Paul's preaching (cf. Rom. ii, 16; 1 Cor. iv, 5; 2 Cor. v, 10) and therefore part of the *Kerygma* (Rom. viii, 31–34).

The Gospel which Paul preached was approved by Peter and James and other Apostles (Gal. ii, 2). His gospel was that of the Apostles, and this gospel included a message concerning Jesus " who was

E

born of the seed of David according to the flesh "
(Rom. i, 3).

In one Epistle Paul possibly refers to Jesus in the
Garden of Gethsemane. " Being obedient even
unto death " (Phil. ii, 8).

When did Paul receive the tradition ? The only
possible occasion was his first visit to Jerusalem,
about seven years after the Crucifixion, that is three
years after his conversion when he stayed with Peter.
Paul's preaching therefore was derived from
Jerusalem.

We turn now to the Acts of the Apostles.
" There is good reason to suppose that the speeches
attributed to Peter in the Acts are based upon
matter which proceeded from the Aramaic-speaking
Church at Jerusalem, and was substantially earlier
than the period at which the book was written."
The sermons of Peter represent the *Kerygma* of the
Church in Jerusalem at an earlier period and these
are to be found in Acts ii, iii, iv, v and x. The
matter of these sermons can be classified as follows:

(1) The Messianic age has dawned. It is now
the age of fulfilment, ii, 16 ; iii, 18, 24.

(2) The coming of the Messianic age has taken
place through the ministry, death, and resurrection
of Jesus. The story of Jesus included :

> His Davidic descent, ii, 30–31.
> His ministry, ii, 22 ; iii, 22 ; x, 34–43.
> His Death, ii, 23 ; iii, 13–14.
> His Resurrection, ii, 24–31 ; iii, 15 ; iv, 10.

(3) By virtue of His resurrection, Jesus has been
exalted to the right hand of God, ii, 33–36; iii, 13 ;
iv, 11.

(4) The holy Spirit in the Church is the sign of Christ's present power and glory, ii, 33 ; v, 32.

(5) Christ will come again, iii, 21.

(6) An appeal for repentance, offer of forgiveness and of the Holy Spirit, ii, 38–39 ; iii, 19, 25–26 ; iv, 12 ; v, 31.

In the sermons in Acts x and xiii, we find the form of preaching when the hearers were Gentiles who did not know the facts of Christ's life. When we compare Peter's preaching to the Roman Cornelius and compare it with Paul's preaching to the men in Antioch of Pisidia, we see that both gave some place to the facts of our Lord's ministry. What events of the ministry are recorded in these two sermons?

" The word . . . preaching the gospel of peace by Jesus Christ," was published " throughout all Judaea." It began in Galilee, included John's baptism, the baptism of Jesus, His acts of " doing good " and of " healing " of which the Apostles were witnesses.

Paul's sermon included references to our Lord's Davidic descent, the preaching of the Baptist, the coming of Jesus, the trial before Pilate, the death and resurrection of Jesus. The sermons are clearly summaries, for they can be read in seven or eight minutes, and we cannot assume that either Peter or Paul delivered such short sermons.

Now what the Apostles preached of the story of the ministry gives very broadly a chronology like that which is to be found in Mark, viz., the preaching of the Baptist, the baptism of Jesus, the preaching and healing in Galilee, the Passion set within " a frame of glory, chapters i–viii, serving as an introduction to the Passion. The theme of Mark is the theme of the *Kerygma* as a whole, ' the beginning of the gospel,' and ' Gospel ' is a virtual equivalent of the *Kerygma*."

The nearer the Gospels are to the *Kerygma*, the nearer we are to the fountain head of the tradition, which was not an interest in facts as mere facts but as facts of saving value to show that God had visited and redeemed His people. " Wherever the Gospels keep close to the matter and form of the *Kerygma*, there we are in touch with a tradition coeval with the Church itself."

(2) *The eye-witnesses in Mark.* The Paradigms are admitted by Dibelius to have been the product of eye-witnesses, who might include Peter, though Dibelius does not say so. Further than this he could not go except for the Passion Narrative, where the evidence of eye-witnesses, e.g., the young man of Mark xiv, is accepted. Reasons for believing that in Mark we find reminiscences of Peter are well known and may be found in all English commentaries. I will only add words which I wrote elsewhere. " The indebtedness of Mark to Peter is well established. It is shown in a very particular way in the Gospel; for there, as we read the record, we almost hear Peter giving his ' testimony '–a phenomenon observable in any revivalist or evangelist campaign. Peter speaks of his failures in the past without reserve and Mark as faithfully reproduces them. Peter the convert may be frequently heard to say, ' Look at what I was and compare it with what I am now, no longer dull, cowardly, traitorous, but a steadfast witness to Christ's power and grace.' The defects of Peter and his fellow apostles are candidly proclaimed in the Gospel, and Peter is

very severe on himself (viii, 32 ff. ; ix, 5–6 ; x, 28–31 ; xiv, 29–37, 66–72). . . . And this unfavourable estimate is also evident in regard to other ' converts,' notably the members of Christ's own family, which included James, the Lord's brother and head of the Church in Jerusalem (iii, 21, 31–32 ; vi, 4). They too had become changed men and women. We may compare this depreciatory and self-condemnatory attitude with that of Paul revealed to us in his accounts of his conversion " (Redlich, p. 134).

Thus the presence of eye-witnesses in Mark's Gospel gives general support for the chronological and biographical details in the record.

(3) *The evidence of Papias.* The internal evidence of Mark is supported by external evidence, the chief of which is that of Papias. An elder, says Papias, used to say that Mark who was Peter's interpreter wrote down accurately, as far as his memory went, what Jesus said or did ; not however in order ($\tau \acute{a} \xi \epsilon \iota$) . . . so that Mark made no error in what he wrote. According to Papias, therefore, Mark was a careful and an accurate historian, though he did not write " in order." What Papias means by " order " is probably grouping in threes or sevens as Matthew did, not historical order. If this is the meaning of the word the evidence of the elder is that Mark's accuracy extends to the historical matter.

Form Critics refuse to accept or utilize the evidence of Papias, and two reasons may be assigned for this attitude. The evidence adduced by Papias is the earliest evidence, outside the Gospels, for the influence of eye-witnesses in the formative period. Also, the statement of the elder was at one time understood to mean that Mark contained nothing

but the reminiscences of Peter whereas it is now
perceived that the elder did not say that Mark wrote
only what was said by Peter or that Peter was
responsible for all that Mark wrote.

R. H. Lightfoot is inclined to disparage the
evidence of Papias. " Until quite lately . . . we
have been glad to avail ourselves of the Papias tradition, according to which St. Mark's record rests,
in part at least, upon the teaching of St. Peter. . . .
It does not seem probable that the Papias tradition
will bear the weight which it is sometimes sought to
lay upon it." Then as to the Marcan Gospel he
says, " The character of this Gospel points, at any
rate for the greater part of its contents, to a different
kind of origin. Internal evidence suggests that
many sections of the narrative have passed through a
' moulding ' process, as it were, before they reached
their present form " (pp. 27 ff.). There follows a
peculiar passage, which is illuminating, for it admits
that Form Critics refuse to consider the evidence of
Papias. Form Criticism, he writes, aims at solving
the problem of the existence of the Gospels " without
any necessary reference to second-century traditions."
This is not a fair approach to the problems raised by
Form Criticism.

(4) *The Marcan Chronology*. We found in the
Acts evidence to prove that the general course of the
ministry of Jesus was a matter of interest to preachers
as well as hearers. We do not and cannot expect
to find a detailed chronology in the Acts, for the
speeches therein are summaries, giving only an
epitome of the sermons and not their complete text.
It is more than probable that the oral tradition
transmitted accounts of our Lord's acts and journeys

as well as of His sayings.   We cannot imagine that
the phrase " doing good " was not expanded, if it
was to convey anything of value to the hearers.

When we turn to Mark we find first of all a broad
outline or basic scheme of the ministry, and secondly,
a certain amount of detail, (*a*) of the ministry in
Galilee, and (*b*) of the Passion.   Mark is not a
biography of Jesus in the modern sense.   It does
not claim to be an exhaustive life of Jesus, but there
is a framework which is both historical and doctrinal.

(i) By the Jordan—the Baptism.   Jesus is revealed to Himself as the beloved Son of God.

(ii) In Galilee—Works of healing and mercy,
teaching on the Kingdom.   Jesus recognized
as Rabbi and Prophet.

(iii) Outside Galilee.   Peter's confession and the
Transfiguration.   Teaching that Jesus is
both Messiah and Saviour, and as Messiah
must suffer and die.

(iv) In Jerusalem.   The Passion and Resurrection proving Jesus is Divine.

The order of the ministry is identical with that in
Acts x, a remarkable corroboration of Peter's connection with the Marcan outline.

Let us next gather together the references to the
ministry in Galilee, setting the contexts in the order
given by Mark.

" Now after that John was delivered up, Jesus came into
Galilee, preaching the gospel of God (i, 14).   And passing
along by the sea of Galilee, he saw Simon and Andrew the
brother of Simon . . . and they followed him (i, 16–18).
And they go into Capernaum; and straightway on the
sabbath day he entered into the synagogue and taught (i, 21).
Jesus could no more openly enter into the city but was

without in desert places (i, 45). And he entered again into Capernaum . . . and he went forth again by the sea side; and all the multitude resorted unto him, and he taught them (ii, 1, 13). And Jesus with his disciples withdrew to the sea : and a great multitude from Galilee followed : and from Judaea, and from Jerusalem, and from Idumaea, and beyond Jordan, and about Tyre and Sidon, a great multitude, hearing what great things he did, came unto him (iii, 7–8). And he goeth up into the mountain and he cometh home (iii, 13, 19 R.V. mg.). And he began to teach by the sea side (iv, 1). And on that day, when even was come, he saith unto them, Let us go over unto the other side (iv, 35). And they came to the other side of the sea, into the country of the Gerasenes (v, 1). They beseech him to depart from their borders (v, 17). And when Jesus had crossed over again in the boat unto the other side, a great multitude was gathered unto him (v, 21). And he went out from thence; and he cometh into his own country ; and his disciples follow him (vi, 1). And he went round about the villages teaching " (vi, 6).

This bare sketch of the ministry of Galilee contains only one generalizing summary, which is clearly Marcan (iii, 7–8). Apart from it, the sketch shows us Jesus journeying up and down Galilee with visits to the sea side and across the sea. There is nothing here to arouse suspicion or doubt but a plain straightforward account of the journeys of Jesus in the province, coherent and natural.

There is thus good evidence to show that in broad outlines Mark gives a reasonable account of Christ's journeys and that his chronology can be respected and accepted. Schmidt's view, on which Assumption Five is based, that the framework of Mark is valueless, is untenable. There is an ordered sequence of events, even though they do not give us a complete itinerary to serve as a basis for a life of Jesus. Mark was interested in chronology and the chronology is of value.

ASSUMPTION SIX. THE ORIGINAL FORM OF THE TRADITION MAY BE RECOVERED AND ITS HISTORY TRACED, BEFORE BEING WRITTEN DOWN, BY DISCOVERING THE LAWS OF THE TRADITION

The synoptic material, claim the Form Critics, can be compared with Rabbinic tradition, Greek literature, folk-lore and the existing Apocryphal literature, and by this means the original form in the pre-literary age before the tradition was changed by Mark can be discovered. Useful information may also be gained by observing the changes made by Matthew and Luke in using Mark, as the knowledge thus obtained will indicate how Mark used the traditional material.

A well-known incident is that of the man, Mark x, 17 ff., who ran to Jesus and knelt to Him and asked Him about eternal life. This man in Luke becomes a ruler (xviii, 18) and in Matthew a young man (xix, 20), whilst in the Apocryphal *Gospel according to the Hebrews* we are told that there were two rich men and that one of them scratched his head when he heard what Jesus required of them.

As an illustration of the laws of the tradition, we may consider that of narrative tradition given by Bultmann.

1. Originally the narratives are:

(*a*) single pictures in simple language;

(*b*) occupy a short period of time, at the most two days, and

(c) as a rule only two speakers or at the most three appear, for complicated stories are beyond the powers of story-tellers.

2. As narratives are retold (a) main facts remain unaltered but details are introduced. For example, the epileptic son in Mark (ix, 17) becomes the only son in Luke (ix, 38); the withered hand in Mark (iii, 1) becomes the right hand in Luke (vi, 6); the ear of the high priest's servant in Mark (xiv, 47) becomes the right ear in Luke (xxii, 50). So also John gives the names Peter and Malchus which are not found in the Synoptics. The conclusion drawn by Bultmann is that names given in Mark are to be doubted.

(b) Indirect statements are turned into direct speech. For example, the following may be compared.

(i) Mark viii, 32.	And Peter took him, and began to rebuke him.
Matt. xvi, 22.	And Peter took him, and began to rebuke him, saying, Be it far from thee, Lord: this shall never be unto thee.
(ii) Mark xiv, 23.	And he took a cup, and when he had given thanks, he gave to them: and they all drank of it.
Matt. xxvi, 27.	And he took a cup, and gave thanks, and gave to them, saying, Drink ye all of it.
(iii) Mark xiv, 1.	Now after two days was the feast of the passover and the unleavened bread.
Matt. xxvi, 1 f.	Jesus said unto his disciples, Ye know that after two days the passover cometh.

(c) There is a schematic idea to turn the unknown

opponents of Jesus into scribes and Pharisees. For example, the " some of them " in Luke xi, 15, are Pharisees in Matthew xii, 34, and scribes in Mark iii, 22. Bultmann's conclusion is that scribes and Pharisees may have been in opposition at times, but that they were " from the outset the sworn enemies of Jesus is certainly unhistorical."

3. If such general laws exist, the claim is made that the length or " worldliness " of a narrative or saying is a guide to date. Dibelius sees a sequence which can be classified according to form. He puts Paradigms first, then Wonder-Stories, then stories about Jesus, then Legends. As Christianity progressively advanced into the world, the stories began to include a secular interest which grew greater with the advance. As for the sayings, Form Critics claim that the short concise sayings preceded the fuller expositions, and in the latter the controversial sayings preceded the parables.

By way of criticism, it may be said that Bultmann's basic assumption that, if we work out the changes made by Matthew and Luke in their use of Mark and Q, we may deduce that the same laws held good even earlier is rather far-fetched. It assumes that as literary men like Matthew and Luke, who may be called scholars, treated literary works, so an unscholarly writer like Mark or a body of unliterary story-tellers would have treated oral tradition. The stylistic methods of writers are no evidence of laws of tradition ; they are indications of the standard of scholarship of the writers.

Again, Form Critics do not allow for the genius of Jesus. Concentrating on forms, they have lost sight of Jesus both as a prophet and as a Rabbi.

Prophets in the Old Testament are given to long discourses and parables, rather than paradigmatic utterances and short epigrams. So with Jesus. The unique character of the parables and their beauty, their emphatic teaching that the kingdom of God had come with the coming of Jesus, their enlargement of the teaching of the law and the prophets, all this is forgotten, and, as a result, the figure of Jesus sinks into the background. The creator of the narratives and sayings becomes a nebulous being.

Further, we question whether the comparison with other literatures is a guide to historical truth. Even if many of the parables of Jesus are founded on other parables, or His sayings are adaptations of pre-existent utterances, or if unliterary men followed the laws of tradition, these do not make the tradition less trustworthy. The genius and personality of Shakespeare are in no way affected by the fact that he made use of existing material. In fact, most Form Critics forget that the religion which turned the world upside down was one based on belief in a Person who truly lived, and died, and rose again, and who spoke as no man ever spoke before. Also, as Bultmann admits that Jesus lived, we fail to understand why the authorship of the parables and sayings should not be assigned to Jesus.

Bultmann, who explains so much by the Christian community, has not explained how and why the living active community existed.

The words of Vincent Taylor are to the point. " We may speak of ' laws of the tradition ' if by these we mean ways in which the minds of those who handed down the tradition had a tendency to act ; but we cannot treat these laws as if they described the work of machines, for there is always an ' unknown quantity ' in the actions of men which defies calculation " (p. 33).   To this warning we may add that it is incredible that stories of Jesus were always presented in a dry impersonal form, as in Paradigms. Sermons would fail to grip and illustrations fail to achieve their end, if vividness of description and the joyfulness of depicting the personality of Jesus were forbidden.   Eastern peoples were not so phlegmatic that they could not be thrilled with a detailed description of a miracle or with the dramatic form of parables or the human appeal of the sick who received sympathy and consideration from the Healer.   The first missionaries preached not only that Jesus lived but that He was a living Jesus.

.   .   .   .   .

We can now sum up the limitations as well as the contributions of Form Criticism in the study of the Gospel tradition.

THE LIMITATIONS OF FORM CRITICISM

1. Classification should be according to form and nothing else, as in Apothegm-Stories, Miracle-Stories and Parables.   Where forms do not exist, classification according to contents is not Form Criticism.

2. " Form "-less groups should not be given historical value—judgments before investigation. Also where a type or form does not exist, no historical valuation can be justified.   Form Criticism should investigate the forms of the tradition, explain the forms, and attempt to trace the development of forms and of forms only.

3. Form Criticism has not made adequate use of the results of Literary Criticism of the Gospels, e.g., the dating of the documentary sources of the synoptic gospels, and the connexion of these sources with the great centres of Christendom.

4. Form Criticism in stressing the influence of the primitive community is blind to the influence of Jesus as a Rabbi and a prophet. On the one hand, it makes the community a creative body, of which there is little or no trace in the New Testament. The primitive Christians were not all Rabbis nor all Solomons. On the other hand, it is not recognized that Jesus was not a teacher who perpetually repeated the same maxims or memorized addresses which He delivered without variation. He is likely to have repeated the same saying in different form and constantly varied His discourses. Also variations in the Gospels may have been due to fuller information. Matthew and Luke and John, who composed their Gospels after Mark, would have been able to revise the narrative from further knowledge.

5. Form Criticism neglects far too much the presence of eye-witnesses in the formative period and their ability to check the tradition and to safeguard it.

6. Form Criticism neglects the evidence of second-century and later writers.

7. Form Criticism has not clearly defined the extent of the formative period.

8. Form Criticism has unjustifiably assumed that the contexts and settings and chronological details are of no historial or biographical value.

9. From Criticism is not justified in assuming

that analogy is a guide to the historical truth of their Legends and Myths.

10. Form Criticism in evaluating the vital factors does not take account of all the varied interests of the early Church.

11. Form Criticism gives a wide scope for subjective treatment and to this its supporters are partial.

12. Form Criticism overlooks the undoubted fact that the primitive Church was willing to suffer and die for its belief in Jesus and the power of His name. Jesus was a real Jesus and their Christ, Who had proved Himself by His deeds and His teaching.

13. Form Criticism by too great an emphasis on the expected Parousia has lost sight of the normal life which men lived though the Parousia was held to be imminent.

THE CONTRIBUTIONS OF FORM CRITICISM

1. Form Criticism by its quest of the *Sitz im Leben*, the life situation, depicts the Church as a living active organism, and strengthens the argument of Literary Criticism that the Gospels took shape under the aegis of a living Church.

2. Form Criticism has proved that in the pre-literary phase of the tradition many narratives of Jesus circulated as self-contained and independent *pericopae*, and that the Passion Narrative was the first to be written down and was based on historic fact.

3. Form Criticism by admitting that collections of sayings were made early has pointed to the possibility that the *ipsissima verba* of our Lord were

treasured as oracles to guide and control the destinies of individuals and of the Church.

4. Form Criticism has shown that very probably certain passages in the Gospels were insertions made by the Church, e.g., the explanations of a few parables said to be given privately were given by the Church when their original significance had been lost or forgotten.

5. Form Criticism has stimulated the study of Gospel origins, and its method of research and investigation may lead to a wider scientific study in the future.

6. Form Criticism, though it has failed to destroy the Marcan order of the narrative, has succeeded in showing that there are gaps in the narrative and that the writing of a modern biography of Jesus, with events in ordered sequence, is not possible. But, on the other hand, there is in broad outline a framework within which the life of Jesus can be surveyed and set.

7. Form Criticism has rightly shown that the early Church was interested in the holy men and women who accompanied our Lord in the days of His flesh.

Chapter III

APOTHEGM-STORIES

THE fundamental characteristic of Apothegm-Stories is a saying or pronouncement of Jesus for which everything else in the narrative serves as a framework (see pp. 27, 51). Many a healing story is of this character; in them, it is the saying and not the miracle which is important.

Another characteristic is the simplicity and brevity of the story. The introduction gives just enough information to make the saying intelligible. It gives no detail. It may consist of a question or answer leading up to the central saying, or may consist of a conventional formula. If the narrative is one of healing, there is no description of the nature of the illness, no description of the process of healing, no technique, no interest in the miracle for its own sake.

The third characteristic is that it should have, what Dibelius terms, an " external rounding off." The narrative must end either with the saying or with an act of Jesus or probably with words giving the effect of the saying.

Two illustrations which show these characteristics at their best may help in understanding them. The first is Christ Blessing the Children.

And they brought unto him little children, that he should touch them: and the disciples rebuked them. But when Jesus saw it, he was moved with indignation, and said unto them, Suffer the little children to come unto me; forbid them not: for of such is the kingdom of God. Verily I say unto you, Whosoever shall not receive the kingdom of God as a little child, he shall in no wise enter therein. And he took them in his arms, and blessed them, laying his hands upon them (Mark x, 13–16).

We notice how bare the details are. There is no description of those who brought the children, no indication of the time or place at which the incident took place ; and the conclusion is short and to the point. The main interest in the story is the utterance of Jesus.

The second illustration may well be one in which a miracle is referred to. Let us take that of the Withered Hand.

And he entered again into the synagogue; and there was a man there which had his hand withered. And they watched him, whether he would heal him on the sabbath day; that they might accuse him. And he saith unto the man that had his hand withered, Stand forth. And he saith unto them, Is it lawful on the sabbath day to do good, or to do harm ? to save a life, or to kill ? But they held their peace. And when he had looked round about on them with anger, being grieved at the hardening of their heart, he saith unto the man, Stretch forth thy hand. And he stretched it forth : and his hand was restored (Mark iii, 1–5).

In this story of healing, the interest is in our Lord's pronouncement on the observance of the Sabbath. The miracle is not described for its own sake or to bring out the power of Jesus. The nature of the cure is not described. Jesus gives an order and it is obeyed. The words and the action of Jesus are here the central point of interest.

These three characteristics are to be found in all Apothegm-Stories, and indicate clearly that the stories circulated as independent single units. This isolation applies even to the stories which were combined in a topical series, as in the five Marcan stories of opposition, of which the last was that of the Withered Hand (see p. 39). Further, in almost all Apothegm-Stories the lack of detail extends to the individuals who are vaguely described; if there is a group of persons, they speak as one and very rarely have a spokesman. This last point may be seen in the story of the Tribute-money.

And they send unto him certain of the Pharisees and of the Herodians, that they might catch him in talk. And when they were come, they say unto him, Master, we know that thou art true, and carest not for anyone: for thou regardest not the person of men, but of a truth teacheth the way of God: Is it lawful to give tribute unto Caesar, or not? Shall we give, or shall we not give? But he, knowing their hypocrisy, said unto them, Why tempt ye me? bring me a penny, that I may see it. And they brought it. And he saith unto them, Whose is this image and superscription? And they said unto him, Caesar's. And Jesus said unto them, Render unto Caesar the things that are Caesar's, and unto God the things that are God's. And they marvelled greatly at him (Mark xii, 13–17).

The introduction is lengthy, but not a single phrase of it is unnecessary. The initial questions and answers lead up to the central answer of Jesus, which has the force of finality on a subject of profound interest. The questioners speak as a united body. Yet there is a problem in the narrative. Do the words " And they marvelled greatly at him " belong to the narrative or are they a Marcan insertion of a kind which is common in Mark? This is, in reality, an illustration of a larger question which may be put thus. Where does an Apothegm-Story end? Dibelius is not always clear on this point, and R. H. Lightfoot is of opinion that " conclusions which point to a larger setting than is afforded by the story itself are unlikely to have formed part of it from the beginning " (p. 47).

The external rounding off.

The conclusions of the Tribute-money and of the plot of the Herodians with the Pharisees (Mark iii, 6) are clearly Marcan insertions and raise no difficulty. But in other cases, the solution is by no means easy. We may consider the questions of Fasting, of the Brethren of Jesus, and of the Anointing.

18, And John's disciples and the Pharisees were fasting: and they come and say unto him, Why do John's disciples and the disciples of the Pharisees fast, but thy disciples fast not? 19, And Jesus said unto them, Can the sons of the bride-chamber fast, while the bridegroom is with them? as long as they have the bridegroom with them, they cannot fast. 20, But the days will come, when the bridegroom shall be taken away from them, and then will they fast in that day (Mark ii, 18–20).

The narrative as it stands is an undoubted Apothegm-Story with the three characteristics clearly shown. But where did the pronouncement of Jesus originally end? Were the two clauses which began " as long as . . ." and " But the days will come . . ." added later by the early Church? Was the original ending 19a or 19, and therefore a pronouncement against fasting? Or is it possible that the Church, having begun to observe a Friday fast, could not let our Lord's pronouncement end where it did, and therefore attributed verse 20 to Him in support of their own practice? Dibelius is convinced that the real content of the story " is decidedly

the defence of a mode of life without fasting."
The words "But the days will come, etc.," he also
thinks, contain a *vaticinium ex eventu* which presup-
poses the passion of Jesus. He admits that this
verse (20) is a typical paradigm ending and witnesses
to its conservative character. "Although the need
was felt of justifying fasting, it was preserved in a
saying of Jesus really of a contrary tendency" (pp.
56 ff.). The passages in verses 19b–20 were a
community-product, according to Bultmann. Vincent Taylor calls this explanation "a study in
historical improbability," and points out that Jesus
made no decisive break with Jewish custom, for in
speaking to the disciples, He said "When ye fast,
be not, as the hypocrites, of a sad countenance."
Taylor, is probably right. It may be, however,
that the fast kept by John's disciples was not a Jewish
fast but one for their dead leader, and they were
asking why the disciples of Jesus would not join in
the observance. Jesus answers that His disciples
still had their Bridegroom with them, but this
would not be for long. The jealousy of John's
disciples is recalled in St. John's Gospel (iii, 22–30).
The Brethren of Jesus raises a similar question
but of a different character.

31, And there come his mother and his brethren; and,
standing without, they sent unto him, calling him. 32, And
a multitude was sitting about him; and they say unto him,
Behold, thy mother and thy brethren without seek for thee.
33, And he answereth them, and saith, Who is my mother
and my brethren? 34, And looking round on them which
sat round about him, he saith, Behold, my mother and my
brethren! 35, For whosoever shall do the will of God, the
same is my brother, and sister, and mother (Mark iii, 31–35.)

Dibelius doubts the historical reliability of the final words, " For whosoever shall do the will of God," etc. They come, he believes, from the preachers who made the Paradigms, since it was necessary to deduce a general principle out of an isolated situation. He similarly considers that the conclusion of the story of Levi, " I came not to call the righteous, but sinners," may also have been the work of preachers who desired to make the words of Jesus in a concrete case applicable to the hearers of the sermons. Here again, we must remember the constructive method of Dibelius. Paradigms were models for sermons, and he finds the two narratives of the Brethren of Jesus and the Call of Levi illustrate his method. The original saying of Jesus can be discovered by getting rid of the edificatory general saying as distinct from the saying to the particular and immediate parties to whom Jesus was speaking. It seems therefore that, as the constructive method is not accepted, the whole story as given in Mark whether of the Brethren of Jesus or the Call of Levi should stand.

The third story which we are to consider as regards its extent is that of the Anointing (Mark xiv, 3 ff.). The discussion relates to the closing words.

8, She hath done what she could: she hath anointed my body aforehand for the burying. 9 And verily I say unto you, Wheresoever the gospel shall be preached throughout the whole world, that also which this woman hath done shall be spoken of for a memorial of her.

The incident, though it occurs in the Passion Narrative, bears all the marks of the type of narrative we are considering, and must have circulated independently. But were the words of verse 8 referring to our Lord's burial a *vaticinium ex eventu* and therefore not part of the Apothegm-Story? If the story, though at first isolated, was always associated with the Passion Narrative, the probability that the words belonged to the original tradition is great. And John who records an Anointing (xii, 1–8), also in Bethany and as part of his Passion Story, though he is evidently supplementing and correcting the Marcan story, mentions the reference to the burial, but omits that of the repetition of the memorial. It is therefore certain that the reference to the burial is historical. On the other hand the final verse about the repetition of the story throughout the world, may be a Marcan insertion; but no final verdict is possible. Taylor thinks that the redactor's hand may be seen in the command for the repetition of the story.

It would seem therefore that the conclusions of Apothegm-Stories, where any doubtful question arises, have to be examined individually. The external rounding off is a true characteristic, but the assumption that if the final words of an Apothegm-Story are general in application, the ultimate clause is due to the preacher, while the penultimate clause is due to Jesus, cannot be accepted. The only safe assumption is that its exact termination is not always certain.

Is there a fourth characteristic?

In some of the stories we have considered, particularly in that of the Anointing and the Brethren of Jesus, a problem of biographical interest arises. Is there a fourth characteristic of Apothegm-

Stories? Should they lack all mention of places
and personal names? Lightfoot says that " it
seems to be true that the Paradigm in its original
form shows no interest in biographical detail."
Dibelius is certain that " the lack of portraiture is a
characteristic of the Paradigms." " The oldest
tradition has no answer to give to questions about
persons belonging to the most intimate circles of
Jesus " (pp. 49 f.).

Dibelius finds only eighteen Paradigms in the
Synoptics, and it is instructive to notice that in the
sixteen of them which are Marcan, the following
give some points of portraiture or the names of
persons—The Brethren of Jesus, the Anointing,
the Call of Levi, Jesus in Nazareth, the Sons of
Zebedee, the Rich Young Ruler, the Blind Man of
Jericho. Of these seven Paradigms, the first two
are amongst those which are of " noteworthy
purity." It would seem that seven out of sixteen
is too large a proportion to enable the conclusion to
be drawn that all Paradigms should lack all mention
of places and persons.

The views of Dibelius on these incidents are
worth considering, even though they are, in some
cases, unworthy of his great scholarship. On the
Brethren of Jesus, Dibelius can only say that the
story does not say " whether the family *always*
hindered Him " ; in the story of Nazareth which is
concerned with His family and in which the names of
the brothers are given, " at least the names of the
sisters are not mentioned." These omissions are to
Dibelius evidence that there is a lack of portraiture
in the Paradigms. He also adduces that the
narrative does not inform us whether Simon the

leper in Bethany was " a sympathetic friend or a lurking enemy." Dibelius is so convinced of this characteristic of his Paradigms that in the story of Bartimaeus, he thinks it probable that this particular Paradigm originally told of the compassion of Jesus for a nameless beggar and that later this nameless beggar was identified with a well-known blind man of Jericho. So also with the Sons of Zebedee ; the narrative may have originally dealt with unnamed persons, but as it stands it shows a real interest in the sons of Zebedee, " although this interest is surely foreign to the Paradigm." Dibelius is quite willing to admit that on occasion even a Paradigm would mention a well-known name.

The story of Zacchaeus and the story of Martha and Mary are not in the list of the Paradigms of Dibelius, for the interest in the former story is in the stature of Zacchaeus, his climbing the tree and his reward, whilst in the latter the names of Martha and Mary are " so ineradicably firm in the words of Jesus " that they cannot be separated from the narrative.

In these problematic cases, the judgment of the student is bound to be subjective. He will have to decide which is more important, the saying or an interest in the persons to whom the narrative refers. If he favours the interest in persons, he will discuss the story under the heading " Stories about holy men and women," the equivalent of the Legenda of Dibelius. But, whatever view may be taken on this particular characteristic, namely, that, which deals with biographical interest, it seems impossible to agree with Dibelius that in this type of narrative " every expression of individual sensibility is absent " and that " *all* the interest " is centred on the saying of Jesus. Even the bare mention of names of well-known persons must have conveyed a special meaning to the narrator and to the Christian Church.

Dibelius gives two further characteristics, both of which are intimately connected with his association of Paradigms with preaching. We need only mention them, for his constructive method has not won the consent of other Form Critics. These two characteristics are (1) " The colouring of the narrative in a thoroughly religious manner." There is no secular touch in any of them and they are " unspoiled," for the narrators did not understand the relations between what they told and the events in the larger world. (2) " The narrative should end in a thought useful for preaching purposes."

Summing up, we may say that the four characteristics of these self-contained units called Apothegm-Stories are the following :

1. The interest is centred in a saying of Jesus or one approved by Him.

2. The narrative is marked by brevity and simplicity. The context of the saying is just enough to make the narrative intelligible.

3. The biographical interest, though lacking in a majority of narratives, forms an ingredient of the Stories. Generally the parties concerned, whether friends or foes, are vaguely described, and the groups rarely have a spokesman and speak as a single body.

4. The narrative generally ends in the saying or in an act of Jesus.

THE APOTHEGM-STORIES

We proceed to take the stories in the Gospels and discuss them, where necessary, and try to ascertain the number of them. The capital letters after each narrative mean that that particular incident is admitted to belong to this type of narrative by the scholars mentioned, A by Albertz, B by Bultmann, D by Dibelius, T by Vincent Taylor. The letter (*b*) within brackets after B means that the narrative belongs to the group which Bultmann calls biographical, and (*c*) after D means that it belongs to Dibelius' group of *Chriae*. In a *Chria*, Dibelius finds that secular interest which is lacking in a Paradigm, and defines it as " a saying ascribed to a particular person and originating from a particular situation." Yet as in a *Chria* the concentration is on the saying, and the *Chriae* are reckoned among the Stories of this type by Bultmann or Taylor we may well discuss them here, and by the symbol (*c*) distinguish them. The letter R after the bracket signifies that in my opinion the narrative is an Apothegm-Story.

We begin with the Gospel according to St. Mark.

i, 16–20. *The Calling of the Disciples* [B (b)].

This is clearly a story in which the interest in the opening verses is centred on Peter and Andrew rather than on the saying. The details are too full, being more than is necessary to form a simple framework for the saying. The story also brings in the call of James and John, though the saying, " Come ye after me, and I will make you to become fishers of men," is not applied to them (see p. 185).

i, 23–27. *The Unclean Spirit* [D].

It is difficult to see why Dibelius calls this miracle a Paradigm. The central point is Jesus' meeting the demoniac and the consequent confirmation of Messiahship, says Dibelius. But as the important sayings in the narrative come not from Jesus but from the unclean spirit and from the bystanders, and there is a reference to the process of the cure, " tearing him and crying with a loud voice," the narrative is a Miracle-Story.

ii, 3–12. *The Sick of the Palsy* [A, B, D, T] R.

It is generally known that a difficulty exists in the Marcan story, and the presence of the parenthetical " he saith unto the sick of the palsy " in verse 10 has suggested the view that this narrative is of composite structure. Two issues are raised in the story, the reality of the forgiveness of the paralytic proved by his being cured, and the right of Jesus to forgive sins. In the first issue, the Jewish theory of the connection of sin with disease and suffering —a theory discussed in *Job*—is raised, and in the second the charge of blasphemy against Jesus, which was one of the causes of opposition against Him. Further, though the central section (vv. 6–10) contains the important pronouncement of Jesus, the story as it stands is a long one and much is described of the man's illness and the effect of the cure. Dibelius sees in the central section " a fictitious conversation." He means that whilst the section is genuine, the opponents say nothing ; all the words are spoken by Jesus, who gives utterance to the thoughts in the hearts of the opponents and answers them. Dibelius therefore considers that there was

an actual protest from the scribes, which brought
forth from Jesus the retort about " which is easier,"
in order to bring the scribes to appreciate the
circumstances aright before He actually healed the
paralytic.

Dibelius may be right, but he has failed to
explain the insertion of the awkward parenthesis in
verse 10.   Taylor has therefore suggested that the
Marcan narrative consists of two distinct stories,
one a Miracle-Story and the other an Apothegm-
Story.   The Miracle-Story can be completely recovered (vv. 3–5a, 11–12).

And they come, bringing unto him a man sick of the palsy,
borne of four.   And when they could not come nigh unto
him for the crowd, they uncovered the roof where he was :
and when they had broken it up, they let down the bed
whereon the sick of the palsy lay.   And Jesus seeing their
faith saith unto the sick of the palsy, I say unto thee, Arise,
take up thy bed, and go unto thy house.   And he arose, and
straightway took up the bed, and went forth before them all ;
insomuch that they were all amazed, and glorified God,
saying, We never saw it on this fashion.

This reconstruction gives us a Miracle-Story with
its three recognized formal characteristics (see p.
52), the nature of the illness, the account of the cure,
and the effect of the cure.   The central section now
becomes an Apothegm-Story which lacks the beginning and the ending, and Taylor suggests that,
before Mark wrote his Gospel, the original introduction and conclusion were cut away and replaced
by the Miracle-Story.   This suggestion seems to
me to be strengthened by the circumstance that the
Miracle-Story and the Apothegm-Story both raise
the common question of forgiveness, and that the

Marcan narrative is the first of a series of five conflict-stories which appear too early in the Gospel and are clearly grouped together on a topical thread (see p. 39).

The incomplete Apothegm-Story (vv. 5b–10) would therefore read thus :

. . . And he saith unto the sick of the palsy, Son, thy sins are forgiven.   But there were certain of the scribes sitting there, and reasoning in their hearts, Why doth this man thus speak ? he blasphemeth : who can forgive sins but one, even God ?   And straightway Jesus, perceiving in his spirit that they so reasoned within themselves, saith unto them, Why reason ye these things in your hearts ?   Whether is easier, to say to the sick of the palsy, Thy sins are forgiven ; or to say, Arise, and take up thy bed, and walk ?   But that ye may know that the Son of man hath power on earth to forgive sins . . .

ii, 15–17.   *Eating with sinners and publicans* [A, B, T] R.   *The Call of Levi* [D].

On the last clause of the last verse " I came not to call the righteous but sinners," see pp. 13, 86, Dibelius says that the parabolic words " They that are whole have no need of a physician, but they that are sick " (17a) were meant to justify the call of Levi, and not the eating with sinners and publicans which were added by Mark.   He therefore calls the Paradigm " The Call of Levi " which includes only Mark ii, 13–14, 17a.   This is very doubtful for the actual story of the Call of Levi ending with " Follow me " is more like a story of Levi.   It is to be noted that the parenthetical clause, " For there were many, and they followed him," refers to the many disciples.

ii, 18–20. *The Question of Fasting* [A, B, D, T] R.

We have already dealt with the extent of this Apothegm-Story (see p. 84). The story as given in Luke definitely connects it with the feast in Levi's house (v, 29) whereas Mark gives it an independent beginning.

ii, 23–27. *The Rubbing of the Ears of Corn* [A, B, T, D] R.

The only question here is whether the words " So that the Son of man is lord even of the sabbath " belong to the narrative.

The problem is complicated by the term " Son of man." Did Jesus use a Messianic term so early in the ministry and before the Confession of Peter? This is doubtful. On the other hand if the term " Son of man " is here the translation of the Aramaic which is capable of meaning " a man," the words might belong to the saying, which would now read " The sabbath was made for man, and not man for the sabbath : so that man is lord even of the sabbath." Again, another explanation is that Jesus used the word " I " and that later the term " Son of man " replaced the first personal pronoun. This would make the saying part of the incident. Rawlinson thinks that the last section of the verse is probably best understood as a Christian comment, " So, then, the Son of man is ' Lord ' even in respect of the Sabbath."

iii, 1–5. *The Withered Hand* [A, B, D, T] R.

Note the vague reference as to place " He entered again into the synagogue." The interest of this narrative is the act of Jesus as well as His saying on the sabbath, which is in the form of a question put by Him to those who watched Him (see p. 82).

iii, 22–30. *The Beelzebub controversy* [A, B, T] R.

Dibelius is quite clear that here isolated sayings, about a house divided, the metaphor of a strong man bound, and a saying on blasphemy, were brought together by the action of a cause preserved in the phrase " because they said, He hath an unclean spirit." This is undoubtedly Mark's own comment and the evangelist, as Dibelius suggests, may have grouped the three sayings, but as he includes them in a narrative framework which gives point to the sayings the whole section can rightly be placed here, for it has all the characteristics of an Apothegm-Story.

Mark has interposed this controversy between two references to the relatives of Jesus. This is not uncommon for other instances in Mark include the story of the Woman with the issue of blood which is woven into the story of Jairus' Daughter, and the Anointing which comes between the plot of the priests and its sequel. The mention of the scandalous tale in Nazareth reminded the evangelist of the blasphemous charge of the scribes from Jerusalem and he dealt with the latter first and then returned to the original incident.

iii, 31–35. *The Mother and Brethren of Jesus* [B (b), D, T] R.

This section should be read with vv. 19b–21 which gives the scandalous rumour current in Nazareth which reached the family of Jesus and set them on their quest. On the final verse see pages 13 and 85.

iv, 10–12. *The Purpose of Parables* [T].

Taylor includes this amongst his Pronouncement-Stories for it has the form of a Pronouncement-Story. " It is not surprising that the Form Critics do not offer this story as a ' paradigm ' or an ' apothegm.' Since Wrede it has been common to explain this passage as a dogmatic addition of Mark in the interests of his view that the Messiahship of Jesus was kept secret during the ministry." It is however possible to accept this section as a view of the early Church which sought to explain why the Jewish nation turned a deaf ear to Christ's teaching. (See p. 156 for a fuller discussion.) The saying comes awkwardly between the parable of the Sower and its explanation which is on different lines and changes the emphasis from the sower to the seed. Dodd, with whom many will agree, asserts that to say that Jesus Himself said that He " clothed His teaching in unintelligible forms, cannot be made credible on any reasonable reading of the Gospels " (pp. 13–15).

vi, 1–4. *The Rejection at Nazareth* [B (b), D] R.

This is clearly an Apothegm-Story which was preserved for the saying " A prophet is not without honour, save in his own country, and among his own kin, and in his own house." The introduction gives information of the kindred of Jesus and states the motive which led to the pronouncement. And the saying ends the narrative. The mention of the name of our Lord's mother and brethren does not satisfy Dibelius, though he allows that occasionally a Paradigm may mention the name of a person. He therefore numbers it amongst those of a less pure type. The fuller narrative in Luke (iv, 16–30) is on the other hand a story about Jesus. Vincent Taylor thinks that the Marcan account is also a story about Jesus.

vii, 5–8. *Clean and Unclean* [A, B, T] R.

Mark has given a long introduction to this pronouncement of Jesus in order to explain the controversy. The original narrative began quite vaguely with verse 5: " And the Pharisees and scribes ask him." Dibelius thinks that vv. 1–5 introduce the whole section which follows as far as v. 23, but he admits that vv. 6–8 are followed by two independent sections dealing respectively with the practice of Corban (9–13) and true cleanliness relating to eating. We may confidently say that Christ's pronouncement in vv. 5–8 is a unit and v. 5 the introduction to it, the occasion which led to it. We thus reckon vv. 5–8 as an Apothegm-Story.

vii, 24–29. *The Syro-Phoenician woman* [B (b)].

Here a saying of the woman is approved by Jesus, who has, in addition, made a pronouncement on which He does not act. It is therefore more likely that the incident was a story about Jesus than one which was preserved for the saying of Christ in it, which was in itself not a guide to conduct or ethics. In the version in Matthew (xv, 21–28), only the words of Jesus and the woman's reply correspond almost exactly. These two verses may however originally have formed part of a story of healing, and been the central section of an Apothegm-Story.

viii, 11–12. *Demand for a Sign* [A, T] R.

This is clearly one of the Apothegm-Stories, an

introduction leading to a pronouncement with which the story concludes.

ix, 38–40. *The Strange Exorcist* [B, T] R.

This has the same construction as the Demand for a Sign.

x, 2–9. *Divorce* [A, B, T] R.

Here the final saying of Jesus is preceded by a question and answer and in all respects the whole section is like the two just referred to above.

x, 13–16. *The Blessing of the Children* [B (b), D T] R.

An Apothegm-Story of the best type. Christ's saying is followed by an appropriate act which forms a perfect " rounding off."

x, 17–22. *The Rich Young Man* [B, D, T] R.

We have already called attention to the variations introduced by Matthew and Luke but the additions that the man was young (Matt.) and a ruler (Luke) may have been suggested by the context. The verses which follow the incident are probably two additional authentic supplements (23–27, 28–31) which Mark attached as pendants to it. They are addressed to the disciples.

x, 35–40. *The Sons of Zebedee* [B, D, T] R.

The problem of portraiture has been referred to (see pp. 87 ff.). Matthew introduces the names of the sons into his version, and thus approximates the narrative to a story of saintly men (a Legend). It is probable that other sayings in vv. 41–45 were attached by Mark, as in the story of the Rich

Young Man. The narrative is undoubtedly interested in the fate of the two brothers but it is not
certain that the prophecy of the death of the brothers
is a *vaticinium ex eventu*. Jesus expected His own
death, and it is historically possible that He foresaw
a like martyrdom of those who were faithful to Him.

x, 46–52. *The Blind Man of Jericho* [D].

Because the names of the beggar and the town are
mentioned Dibelius calls this a Paradigm of a less
pure type. There is no special saying of Jesus in
the narrative which, on the other hand, is of biographical interest. It mentions the beggar's name,
the city which is associated with the story, and
describes the action of the blind man who cast away
his garment, sprang up, and came to Jesus, and gives
the persistent cry of the blind man and the saying of
the spectators. As a story of Bartimaeus the narrative takes its most suitable place.

xi, 12–14, 20–22. *The Withered Fig Tree* [B].

To the conclusion of the Cursing of the Fig-tree,
Mark has appended two sayings about faith and a
mountain (v. 23) and prayer (v. 24). The saying
on faith is found in slightly different form in other
contexts (Matt. xvii, 20; Luke xvii, 6) which are set
round the thought of a grain of mustard seed, and in
Luke the saying is addressed not to the mountain
but to a sycamine tree. It looks therefore as if the
answer of Jesus to the remark that the fig tree was
withered consisted only of the phrase " Have faith in
God." The whole incident in this case would be a
Miracle-Story (vv. 12–14, 20–22). Many scholars
think that the miracle probably grew out of a parable.

But the question must be left an open one for lack of information.

xi, 15–17. *The Cleansing of the Temple.* [B (b), D] R.

Dibelius says that this is a Paradigm and that v. 18, " and the chief priests and the scribes heard it, and sought how they might destroy him . . ." is not part of the Paradigm for it does not make " an external rounding off." It goes beyond the moment of cleansing and refers to the whole period of the visit to Jerusalem. This verse is clearly a Marcan commentary on the situation following the cleansing. The incident in other respects, if confined to vv. 15–17, has all the characteristics of an Apothegm-Story.

xi, 27–33. *The Question of Authority* [A, B, T] R.

A clear Apothegm-Story which probably began at v. 28, " They said unto him."

xii, 13–17. *The Question of the Tribute-Money* [A, B, D, T] R.

A perfect example of an Apothegm-Story, questions and answers leading on naturally to our Lord's dictum. The questioners are vaguely described and speak as a united body without a spokesman (see p. 83).

xii, 18–27. *The Question of Resurrection* [A, B, D, T] R.

This like the preceding question on Tribute-Money formed an independent unit and was probably included in a topical series of conflict stories (see p. 39). The introduction is short, " And there come unto him Sadducees, which say that there

is no resurrection." The barest information is
given of the beliefs of the sect, but it is all that is
needed to give point to the narrative.

xii, 28–31. *The Great Commandment* [A, B, D (c),
T] R.

The comparison of the Marcan story with the
parallel versions in Matthew and Luke is instructive
for the latter Gospels omit three verses (29, 32, 33)
and the first part of 34, and there are other differences.
It is possible therefore that the original story
consisted only of the first four verses.

xii, 35–37. *The Davidic Sonship* [A, T] R.

This is in form similar to the incomplete Apothegm-
Story in the Sick of the Palsy, in that both question
and answer are given by Jesus.   In Matthew it is
in the form of a conversation.

xii, 41–44. *The Widow's Mite* [B (b), T] R.

This incident bears all the marks of an Apothegm-
Story.   Dibelius suggests that the narrative may be
traced to a saying of Jesus and " especially to a
parable."   He means that Mark supplied the framework.   Bultmann does not believe in the story.
How could Jesus have known what the widow
contributed?

xiii, 1–2. *The Fall of Jerusalem* [B (b), T] R.

We have to decide whether this is a *vaticinium ex
eventu* or a historical utterance.   No reason can be
shown why it should be a prophecy after the event
for genuine similar prophecies are to be found in
Old Testament prophecy.

xiv, 3–9. *The Anointing in Bethany* [B (b), D, T) R.

The extent of this Apothegm-Story has been questioned. Dibelius objects to the references to the burial and the future remembrance of the story, which he calls " a pragmatic ending."

She hath done what she could: she hath anointed my body aforehand for the burying. And verily I say unto you, Wheresoever the gospel shall be preached throughout the whole world, that also which this woman hath done shall be spoken of for a memorial of her.

The reference to the memorial may be a later insertion for the words " preach the Gospel " enshrine a later idea belonging to a missionary Church, and if the incident, originally a *pericope*, was attached to the Passion Story for purposes of worship in the Church the fulfilment would have already taken place. But the reference to the burial is quite in keeping with thoughts of our Lord's approaching death which were present in the days preceding the Passion. No dogmatic conclusion is possible however (see p. 86).

. . . . .

We now turn to Q, the non-Marcan matter common to Matthew and Luke. We find four sections which must be considered.

Luke iv, 1–13: *The Temptation* [A]R.

Is this a story of Jesus or are three independent Apothegm-Stories combined? Or should we with Bultmann and Dibelius call the whole section a Myth?

Both Matthew and Luke give us three temptations, all of which took place in the wilderness,

But there is a possibility that the three temptations described in Q did not take place at the same time. That of the offer of the kingdoms of the world may very well and suitably have been associated with the occasion when, after the feeding of the 5,000, the people tried to force a kingship on Jesus. That of the Pinnacle of the Temple in Jerusalem may have been a severe temptation, on the way to Jerusalem, to save Himself from the Cross. It suits the time when the disciples were amazed and were afraid (Mark x, 32), or it may have followed the Transfiguration (see p. 195). This theory that whilst the first temptation was clearly connected with the wilderness, the other temptations came at other crises in our Lord's ministry is supported by the fact that Matthew and Luke give the two in different order. If then the three temptations came at three distinct intervals of time, the accounts of them might have circulated as independent units and been united on a topical thread. Albertz therefore may be right in holding that Q gives three independent controversial narratives in a group, each containing just sufficient framework to make the central sayings intelligible.

The circumstance that the controversy takes place between the supernatural Jesus and a supernatural demon leads Dibelius to call the Temptation a myth. This designation will come up for discussion in a later chapter.

Luke vii, 6b–9. *The Centurion's servant* [B (b)] R.

Matthew and Luke, whilst they differ in the details of the narrative, agree on the message of the centurion and the reply of Jesus. It is therefore possible

that Luke and Matthew supplied editorial additions
to an incident retained in Q for the value of the
sayings of the centurion and of Jesus. If the words
common to the narrative portions are collected we
get a perfect Apothegm-Story which reads as
follows, if we follow the Lucan version.

He entered into Capernaum. And a centurion, whose
servant was sick, sent friends to him, saying unto him, Lord
I am not worthy that thou shouldest come under my roof:
wherefore neither thought I myself worthy to come unto
thee: but say the word and my servant shall be healed.
For I also am a man under authority, having under myself
soldiers: and I say to this one, Go, and he goeth; and to
another, Come, and he cometh; and to my servant, Do this,
and he doeth it. And when Jesus heard these things, he
marvelled at him, and turned and said unto the multitude that
followed him, I say unto you, I have not found so great faith,
no, not in Israel.

The incident was valued for the sayings and not as
a miracle. No word of healing is pronounced by
Jesus, but only words commending the centurion's
faith. It is possible that Q contained a statement of
the cure but the conclusions differ in Matthew
and Luke, though they agree that the servant was
healed. The absence of a statement about the cure
prevents the incident from being grouped amongst
the Miracle-Stories. On the other hand, the
narrative as given above contains all the characteristics of the group under review.

Luke vii, 19–23. *The Question of John the Baptist*
[A, B, T] R.

The only difficulty is the Lucan verse which
comes between the message of John and our Lord's

reply : " In that hour he cured many of diseases and plagues and evil spirits ; and on many that were blind he bestowed sight." Now Matthew omits this verse and the preceding. But they agree almost identically in the message of John and the reply. It is therefore more than likely that the version in Q did not contain the two verses referred to, namely, vv. 20 and 21, and that the version in Q was an Apothegm-Story which began, " And John sent two of his disciples, and said unto him, Art thou he that cometh, or look we for another? And he answered and said, Go your way, and tell John," etc.

Luke ix, 57–62. *The Candidates for Discipleship* [B (b), T] R.

Possibly three independent *pericopae* grouped round a common theme. Matthew gives only two of them and assigns the first question to a scribe. Luke's version is that the three questions were put on one occasion.

.   .   .   .   .

We now proceed to examine possible Apothegm-Stories in the narratives peculiar to Luke, which came from his special source L. Dibelius finds eight *Chriae* in L, and holds that five of them contain a situation artificially created by Luke. A good example of a *Chria* may be found in the incident of the woman who called down a blessing on the mother of Jesus.

After Luke vi, 4. *The man working on the sabbath* [D (c), T] R. in Codex Bezae.

He saw a man working on the sabbath and said unto him, Man if thou knowest what thou art doing thou art blessed ;

but if thou knowest not, thou art accursed and a transgressor of the law.

It reads like a genuine piece of tradition and has the characteristics of an Apothegm-Story. There are other stories in this group which deal with sabbath observance.

vii, 36–50. *The Sinful Woman in Simon's House* [B].

The incident as it stands is too long and too involved to be an Apothegm-Story. If, as is thought by some scholars, the Parable of the two debtors and the saying belonging to it should be removed, we get a form which is more like that of an Apothegm-Story. If the Parable is a constituent part of the incident, the parable teaches that the woman loved Jesus before she had been forgiven. If it is omitted, the incident would mean that she received forgiveness because of her love. The story as it stands is rightly classed by Dibelius amongst stories of holy men and women.

ix, 52b–55. *The Samaritan Village* [B, D].

The problem here is complicated by the text. The Revised Version in the text which follows reads vv. 54 and 55 without the words in brackets, which, it says in the margin, are given by some ancient authorities.

54, And when his disciples James and John saw this, they said, Lord, wilt thou that we bid fire to come down from heaven, and consume them (even as Elijah did)? 55, But he turned, and rebuked them (and said, ye know not what manner of spirit ye are of, for the Son of man came not to destroy men's lives, but to save them).

If the words within brackets belong to the text, the narrative is an Apothegm-Story. Without them, there is no saying of Jesus in response to the fiery request of the Sons of Thunder, but only the words of the narrative, " He turned and rebuked them," which Dibelius calls a " colourless remark." He also suggests further that perhaps the manuscripts inserted the words within brackets in accordance with true expectation and that the same narrator gave the names James and John to two disciples hitherto unnamed.

x, 38–42. *Martha and Mary* [B (b)].

The saying of Jesus is very familiar for His view on domestic happiness but, as Dibelius says, the names of the sisters are inseparably connected with the incident and the details are very full and give more information than an Apothegm-Story should. It is in the women rather than in the saying that the interest of the story probably lies.

xi, 27–28. *The Blessing of the Mother of Jesus* [B (b), D (c), T] R.

It has been suggested that this is a variant tradition of the Relatives of Jesus in Mark (iii, 31–35). It may be so, but that question does not concern us here.

xii, 13–15. *Dividing the Inheritance* [B, D (c), T] R.
xiii, 1–5. *The Murdered Galilaeans* [B, D (c), T] R.
xiii, 11–17. *The Bent Woman* [B, T].

The details of the story are given in full, there is a discussion between the ruler of the synagogue and Jesus, and the saying of Jesus about the sabbath is specifically related to the illness of the woman " whom Satan had bound eighteen years." There is a laying on of hands. The main interest seems to be in the woman and not in the saying on the sabbath. The conclusion too refers to the "glorious things" done by Jesus. It is probable that originally there was a simpler form of the story which was an Apothegm-Story. Dibelius calls this story a "hybrid form." It is certainly not as simply described as two other Apothegm-Stories which are concerned with the sabbath, viz., the Withered Hand and the Dropsical Man.

xiii, 31–32. *Jesus and Herod* [B (b), D (c)] R.

A saying of Jesus of interest, in matters of state, to the Christians. Dibelius thinks the introduction was artificial and inserted by Luke.

xiv, 1–5. *The Dropsical Man* [B, D, T] R.

xvii, 11–19. *The Ten Lepers* [B (b)].

The interest here lies in the story itself, particularly in the gratitude of the Samaritan.

xvii, 20–21. *The Coming of the Kingdom* [B, D (c), T] R.

xix, 1–10. *Zacchaeus* [B (b)].

A story of Zacchaeus for it describes his stature, his climbing the sycamore tree, his haste in coming down from it, and his sign of repentance. It is clearly not an Apothegm-Story.

xix, 39–40. *The Rejoicing of the Disciples* [B (b), D (c)] R.

xix, 41–44. *The Weeping over Jerusalem* [B (b), D (c)] R.

The introductions in these two sections may be artificial, but they are probably authentic.

xxiii, 27–30. *The Weeping Women* [B (b), T] R.

A saying of Jesus of an eschatological character,

important in view of the coming Parousia. The
narrative is in keeping with the saying and the
occasion of its utterance.

.   .   .   .   .

We are left with Matthew and John. One
Apothegm-Story is to be found in the first Gospel.

Matt. xvii, 24–26. *The Temple Tax of the Half-
shekel* [B (b), T] R.

This incident, because of the addition of the
miracle of the coin in the fish's mouth in verse 27,
has generally been admitted to be a legend, that
is in the English sense of a story with no basis of
fact. But Form Criticism has helped to recognize its value, for as an Apothegm-Story the interest
in primitive Christianity lay not in the miracle but
in its pronouncement. It enshrined a saying of
Jesus that Christians were to pay the tax to the
Temple, though the sons of the kingdom were free.
The story is complete without the miracle.

In the Gospel according to St. John, there is one
assured Apothegm-Story, and two possible others,
and another in the *pericope* omitted by most ancient
authorities.

ii, 14–16. *The Cleansing of the Temple* [D] R.

Dibelius omits this in his tabular list because it is a
parallel to the synoptic story of the same event.
John places the incident early in his Gospel, but
Dibelius remarks that we have " the rare case that
an event has been handed down in two different
Paradigms." This may be due to the pre-eminent
position assigned to the Passion Story.

vii, 53—viii, 11. *The Woman taken in Adultery* [T] R.

This independent unit, though recognized not to be part of the Johannine Gospel is found in the group of texts known as Fam. 13 where it follows Luke xxi, 38 ; also in the group Fam. 1, it is found at the end of John in manuscript 1 of the group. The actual story was evidently valued for its bearing on the problem of unchastity. Dibelius, though he quoted the story of the Man working on the Sabbath as a Paradigm, does not include the Woman taken in Adultery though it too is found in the Latin Codex.

The narrative is certainly an Apothegm-Story, and fulfils all its requirements.

Two other possible Apothegm-Stories can be suggested, but, owing to the difficulties of interpretation, no final conclusion can be drawn. In the texts given below, they possess the characteristics of the type, but there is no guarantee that the actual event ended at the verses with which the stories are here concluded.

x, 22–25. *Art thou the Christ?*

And it was the feast of the dedication at Jerusalem : it was winter ; and Jesus was walking in the temple in Solomon's porch. The Jews therefore came round about him, and said unto him, How long dost thou hold us in suspense ? If thou art the Christ, tell us plainly. Jesus answered them, I told you, and ye believe not : the works that I do in my Father's name, these bear witness of me.

xiii, 12–14. *Washing the Disciples' Feet*

So when he had washed their feet, and taken his garments, and sat down again, he said unto them, Know ye what I have done to you ? Ye call me Master and Lord : and ye say

well; for so I am.   If I then, the Lord and the Master, have
washed your feet, ye also ought to wash one another's feet.

.   .   .   .   .

Dibelius assigns to his list of Paradigms eighteen
incidents in the synoptic Gospels, ten of which
being of a less pure type must have their accretions
removed before we can hope to obtain the original
Paradigm.   In his opinion, the Paradigms are on
the whole trustworthy and are so because they were
used for preaching, which, we must remember,
included the teaching of catechumens.   Perhaps he
would allow that, even if his constructive method
failed to convince us, that his eighteen stories are
relatively trustworthy.   It is however doubtful
whether he would extend the verdict to all the
forty-three Apothegm-Stories in the list above. His
division into two groups is open to criticism. For
example the Rubbing of the Ears of Corn is in his
pure group and the call of Levi in his less pure
group, but he only objects to the inclusion of a
paragraph in each, not to the presence of the
personal name Levi.   Other criticisms have already
been made on this matter at the beginning of this
chapter.

Bultmann however is very sceptical.   He divides
his Apothegms into two groups, (a) controversial
and (b) biographical.   Apothegms, he says, are
found in Jewish as well as in Greek literature but
there were characteristic differences.   In Jewish
literature the saying, given as an answer to a question, usually appears as a counter question and those
Gospel Apothegms of this form were therefore
formulated in a Jewish environment.   On the
other hand, the influence of Greek Apothegms are

to be seen in those Gospel narratives which begin with a conventional formula such as " When he was asked," " When he observed."

In the controversial Apothegms, which starts with some act of Jesus or the disciples followed by an attack on their conduct and finally by Christ's answer, the chief issues raised were those which affected the Christian community. The ritual observations show that they arose in the community ; the Christians were defending their break with traditional law by stories which appealed to a pronouncement of Jesus.

The biographical Apothegms, of which there are twenty, are mainly creations of the community " since they give expression to what Christians experienced of their Master or what He experienced at the hands of the people." They are probably ideal situations since they express a symbol or ideal and not the actual situation. For example, the Visit to Nazareth gives a symbolic picture setting forth the attitude of people generally to the preaching of Jesus.

Bultmann, therefore, finds the narratives mostly unhistorical but the sayings in many cases may be historical. The scene in the majority of cases has grown round the saying to explain it. Of the genuine Apothegms two are the Tribute-Money, and the Anointing.

We must acknowledge the skill of Bultmann in tracing the parallelism with Rabbinic and Hellenistic Apothegms. But he has overlooked the Hellenistic influence in Palestine which came about the time of the Maccabees. The presence of Hellenistic Christians in the early Christian community is

H

attested in the Acts of the Apostles and it was a problem connected with Greek widows that led the Apostles to appoint seven men of ability and good report to superintend the work of relief.

Again, "controversial" is not a suitable term. Sometimes we find only a question and answer, often put by enemies as well as friends. However, it is not the title which is of immediate interest but the assumption of Bultmann that nearly every Apothegm received its narrative portion from the imaginative skill of the community. We have already seen that the questions raised in the Apothegms are rarely those which arose from the life-situation of the early Church but those which were living issues during our Lord's ministry. To recall one example, the question of Sabbath observance was quite a secondary issue in the early Church but was a cause of conflict between Jesus and the scribes (see pp. 55 ff.). In short, the Apothegm-Stories are a reflection of the actual conditions of the days Jesus preached in Palestine. We must remember that Bultmann does not deny that Jesus ever lived. He forgets that Jesus did not live in isolation and that, as One who uttered historical *apothegmata*, He was attended by eye-witnesses anxious to hear and learn the words of wisdom which fell from the Rabbi's lips. To expect our Lord's hearers to forget every occasion but two, and when and in what circumstances every pronouncement was made is to expect the incredible.

Chapter IV

MIRACLE-STORIES

THE miracles, except those which were included under Apothegm-Stories, possess certain common characteristics. Here we see another of the contributions of Form Criticism in the recognition not only that the Miracle-Stories circulated as self-detached units but also that they possess a common literary structure. We shall have to use the term Miracle-Stories, though it fails to express the characteristics of the group, because of the difficulty of suggesting a better. "Form-Miracles" is the ideal term, but like nature-miracles, might suggest that the miracles are miracles which deal with forms as nature-miracles deal with nature. A term that has been suggested is Wonder-Stories, but this is not as useful as Miracle-Stories, because of the emphasis placed on the wonder evoked by Christ's works of healing and power. We shall later show reason to hold that wonder is not the only idea which has to be emphasized.

Dibelius uses the term Novellen or Tales but the title is unsatisfactory, for by Novelle he means a short story of a miracle written with formal characteristics, which is certainly not the meaning of a Novelle pure and simple.

The fundamental structural characteristics of all miracles are threefold—the illness or necessity or danger is described, the trouble is averted, and the effect of the miracle is finally stated. We shall consider these in detail presently.

Now, in the Apothegm-Stories, a number of miracles were included because the predominant value of their narratives was in the saying. In their framework there was no attempt to describe the miracle itself at any length, nor was the effect of the miracle usually part of the narrative. It ended generally in the pronouncement of Jesus or an act of His. In contrast with the Apothegm-Stories, Miracle-Stories are not brief and simple but full of detail, the interest of each is in the miracle for its own sake even though a word of Jesus is present in the narrative, and the conclusion of each is the cure and the effect produced instead of a saying or act of Jesus. Miracles classed under Apothegm-Stories were the Sick of the Palsy (the central portion vv. 5b–10), the Withered Hand, the Centurion's Servant, and the Dropsical Man. We also discussed the Unclean Spirit, the Syro-Phoenician Woman, Blind Bartimaeus, the Withered Fig Tree, the Bent Woman, and the Ten Lepers, each of which was reckoned either as an Apothegm or Paradigm by Bultmann or Dibelius. The Syro-Phoenician story probably was originally an Apothegm-Story.

The Miracle-Stories proper consist therefore of the following, of which eighteen are healing-miracles and six are nature-miracles. The healing-miracles include :

The Unclean Spirit in the synagogue (Mark i, 23–27).

Peter's Wife's Mother (Mark i, 30–31).

The Leper (Mark i, 40–45).

The Sick of the Palsy (the narrative portion) (Mark ii, 3–5a, 11, 12).

The Gerasene Demoniac (Mark v, 1–20).

The Daughter of Jairus (Mark v, 21–24, 35–43).

The Woman with the Issue of Blood (Mark v, 25–34).

The Deaf and Dumb Man (Mark vii, 31–37).

The Blind Man of Bethsaida (Mark viii, 22–26).

The Epileptic Boy (Mark ix, 14–29).

Blind Bartimaeus (Mark x, 46–52).

The Dumb Demoniac (Q. Luke xi, 14).

The Widow's Son at Nain (Luke vii, 11–17).

The Ten Lepers (Luke xvii, 11–19).

The Nobleman's Son (John iv, 46–54).

The Lame Man at the Pool of Bethesda (John v, 1–9).

The Man Born Blind (John ix, 1–7).

The Raising of Lazarus (John xi, 1–46).

The six nature-miracles are :

The Stilling of the Tempest (Mark iv, 35–41).

The Feeding of the Five Thousand (Mark vi, 32–44, John vi, 1–13).

The Walking on the Sea (Mark vi, 45–52 ; John vi, 15–21).

The Cursing of the Fig Tree (Mark xi, 12–14, 20).

The Draught of Fishes (Luke v, 1–11).

The Changing of Water into Wine (John ii, 1–11).

The first question to be discussed is whether each of these Miracle-Stories circulated independently. The answer to this depends on the beginning and con-clusion of the stories. It is generally admitted that the Raising of Jairus' Daughter and the Woman with the Issue of Blood were always a unit, and that the insertion of the latter story between the appeal of

Jairus and our Lord's entry into the ruler's house is not artificial. Again, the series in Mark iv, 35—v, 43, of which the above-mentioned pair form part, include the Stilling of the Tempest and the Gerasene Demoniac, and this cycle was very probably connected originally. Another connected pair is certainly that of the Feeding of the Five Thousand and the Walking on the Sea. Even John does not separate them. The notice of time, "when the even was come," is too strong a part of the narrative to be discarded. Dibelius can only say that " it is very difficult to be certain on the point."

The opening words of the narratives have only been questioned in one instance, namely, in Mark iv, 36, which clearly refers back to the boat mentioned in iv, 1, and is editorial. The inclusion of the verse does not however raise the question of the independent circulation of the Walking on the Sea or of the cycle of which it probably formed a part.

The conclusions of some of the narratives are questioned by Form Critics on the ground that they contradict Wrede's theory of the Messianic secret (see pp. 19 ff.). Is the conclusion to be merely the confirmation of the cure shown by the effect on the onlookers or does it include Christ's request for secrecy? Are the requests to keep silence Marcan " remarks of a pragmatic character"? But whether the prohibitions of Jesus are accepted as parts of the original tradition or not, there is in all cases a " complete rounding off."

Thus the Miracle-Stories, with the certain exception of two sets of two miracles each—Jairus' Daughter with the Woman with the Issue, and the Five Thousand with the Tempest—may be said to

be self-detached units which originally circulated
independently.

THE FORMAL CHARACTERISTICS

1. The miracle dominates everything, and the
saying, if any, is of secondary interest. Each
miracle, as we have said, possesses three elements.
Two illustrations of healing-miracles may be considered, one including the command for secrecy
but both showing the characteristics. The Sick
of the Palsy is the first. It begins with the circumstances, which led to the paralytic being placed
before Jesus, the difficulties which were overcome,
and the faith of the sick man and the bearers:

And they come, bringing unto him a man sick of the
palsy, borne by four. And when they could not come nigh
unto him for the crowd, they uncovered the roof where he
was: and when they had broken it up, they let down the bed
whereon the sick of the palsy lay.

The cure is next described:

And Jesus seeing their faith saith unto the sick of the
palsy, I say unto thee, Arise, take up thy bed, and go unto
thy house.

Finally comes the effect of the cure:

And he arose, and straightway took up the bed, and went
forth before them all; insomuch that they were all amazed,
and glorified God, saying, We never saw it on this fashion.

Our second illustration is the Healing of a Leper
(Mark i, 40–45). First, the circumstances are
described, including the suppliant attitude of the
leper:

And there cometh to him a leper, beseeching him, and

kneeling down to him, and saying unto him, If thou wilt,
thou canst make me clean.

The cure follows.   We notice the action of the hands
of Jesus :

And being moved with compassion, he stretched forth
his hand, and touched him, and saith unto him, I will; be
thou made clean.

The conclusion included the charge laid on the leper
by Jesus :

And he strictly charged him, and straightway sent him out,
and saith unto him, See thou say nothing to any man : but
go thy way, shew thyself to the priest, and offer for thy
cleansing the things which Moses commanded, for a testimony unto them.

The nature-miracles show the common elements of
structural form.   Let us take as an illustration the
Stilling of the Tempest (Mark iv, 35–41).   The
narrative opens with a description of the circumstances which led to the dangerous situation, which
itself is described with vivid touches.

And on that day, when even was come, he saith unto them,
Let us go over unto the other side.   And leaving the multitude, they take him with them, even as he was, in the boat.
And other boats were with him.   And there ariseth a great
storm of wind, and the waves beat into the boat, insomuch
that the boat was now filling.   And he himself was in the
stern, asleep on the cushion : and they awake him, and say
unto him, Master, carest thou not that we perish ?

The assuaging of the storm follows and the words
used by Jesus are in the nature of a formula with
which He rebukes the spirit, which was held in
those days to have caused the storm :

And he awoke, and rebuked the wind, and said unto the
sea, Peace, be still.

Lastly, we read of the result of Christ's words on the sea, and the effect produced on the disciples :

And the wind ceased, and there was a great calm. And he said unto them, Why are ye fearful ? have ye not faith ? And they feared exceedingly, and said one to another, Who then is this, that even the wind and the sea obey him ?

Other characteristics of Miracle-Stories to be noted have already been mentioned but are well worth repeating.

2. The circumstances leading up to the miracle are often given in great detail and there is an interest in the details for their own sake. In the Raising of Jairus' Daughter, the introduction takes ten verses out of thirteen. In the Woman with the Issue of Blood, the failure of the doctors to cure her is described in order to enhance the power of Jesus and the faith of the patient : " And a woman, which had an issue of blood twelve years, and had suffered many things of many physicians, and had spent all that she had, and was nothing bettered, but rather grew worse, having heard the things concerning Jesus, came in the crowd behind, and touched his garment. For she said, If I touch but his garments, I shall be made whole." In the Epileptic Boy, the failure of the disciples to cure him is reported, and the nature of the illness is very realistically described. " I brought unto thee my son, which hath a dumb spirit ; and wheresoever it taketh him, it dasheth him down : and foameth, and grindeth his teeth, and pineth away . . . and oft times it hath cast him both into the fire and into the waters, to destroy him." The Wedding in Cana, the Raising of Lazarus and others show the general difference

between Miracle-Stories and Apothegm-Stories. The Miracle-Stories are of interest in themselves. This is not always due to the length of the description, for the cure of Peter's wife's mother, though a very short Miracle-Story, is framed according to the structural laws of this group.

> Now Simon's wife's mother lay sick of a fever ; and straightway they tell him of her.

This is followed by the cure :

> And he came and took her by the hand, and raised her up ; and the fever left her.

Then comes the effect of the cure in the words :

> And she ministered unto them.

3. Thirdly, unlike the Apothegm-Stories, the words of Jesus are relatively few, apart from the words which precede or accompany the action. In the cure of the leper, His words are an injunction to secrecy (Mark i, 40). Then we have " Why are ye fearful ? have ye not yet faith ? " (iv, 40). " Fear not, only believe " (v, 36). " Be of good cheer : it is I, be not afraid " (vi, 50). To the blind man after he is cured, Jesus says, " Do not even enter into the village " (viii, 26). To the father of the epileptic boy, " This kind can come out by nothing, save by prayer " (ix, 29). In the Ten Lepers, " Were not the ten cleansed ? but where are the nine ? Were there none found that returned to give glory to God, save this stranger ? " (Luke xvii, 18). The few stories in John contain a number of sayings.

4. Fourthly, frequent references in Mark contain statements depreciating our Lord's influence on others or derogatory of the conduct and ignorance

of the Apostles. Our Lord forbids the leper to make his cure public but the leper goes out and begins to publish it much (i, 45). The Gerasene demoniac dares to adjure Jesus, " I adjure thee by God, torment me not " (v, 7). This is in keeping with other passages in the Gospel where even the Person of Christ is called in question, " Is not this the carpenter? " (vi, 3). " Why callest thou me good? none is good save one, even God " (x, 13). Matthew and Luke omit or alter these passages.

With regard to the Apostles, they are represented as distrustful. " Master, carest thou not that we perish? " (iv, 38). "And sayest thou, Who touched me? " (v, 31). Matthew and Luke modify or omit these questions.

5. Fifthly, Faith is a frequent element in the narratives, personal faith in Jesus and also a faith in His miraculous power. We shall deal with this later.

6. Lastly, the conclusions frequently refer to the amazement caused by the healings or by our Lord's power over nature. John's Gospel is practically lacking in this characteristic.

There are other points of interest in these Miracle-Stories, though they do not point to any formal characteristics.

We notice in the miracles a partiality for numbers. Five thousand are fed with five loaves and two fishes and there are twelve baskets to collect the remnants. The bread would have cost 200 denarii. The multitude sat down in ranks, by 100's and by 50's. Jairus' daughter was twelve years old, and the woman with an issue had suffered twelve years; it was the fourth watch when Jesus walked on the sea; there were six waterpots at Cana each holding two or three firkins; there were about 2,000 pigs which rushed into the sea and were drowned; Lazarus had been dead for four days; 153 fish were caught in fishing on the Sea of Galilee.

Again we notice that the words of cure are given, and Form Critics compare them to the magical formulas of other nations, and call attention to the fact that Mark often gives the Aramaic words used by Jesus. Ephphatha, Talitha cumi, " Peace be still," " I will, be thou clean." Or there are descriptions of the methods of cure. There is the touch of Jesus as in the Epileptic Boy, the Widow's Son at Nain, the Deaf and Dumb Man, the Blind Man. In the Deaf and Dumb Man, Jesus sighs and looks up to heaven. In the Raising of Lazarus, He lifts up His eyes. In some cases, spittle is used as a medium for the cure as in the healing of the deaf and dumb man, and of the blind man. Now, some Form Critics see in the technique thus described guidance given to help Christians who possessed the gift of healing. The end of the Epileptic Boy, says Dibelius, is " a recipe," for the future cure of such cases. "This kind can come out by nothing save by prayer (and fasting)." Others, like Bultmann, see in them proofs that the miracles are simply based on similar miracles described in non-Christian literature. They are therefore unhistorical.

Two of the synoptic healing-stories need some consideration. The first is the Widow's Son at Nain. Has the original event received later insertions? The difficulty is connected with the presence of the widow at the funeral. The designation is mentioned at the beginning but that is no reason for assuming that she accompanied the procession to the grave. If the verse, " And when the Lord saw her, he had compassion on her, and said unto her, Weep not," and the phrase " And he gave him to his mother " were removed, the story would give a good tradition. The difficulty is recognized by other than Form Critics.

And it came to pass soon afterwards, that he went to a city called Nain; and his disciples went with him, and a great multitude. Now when he drew near to the gate of the city, behold, there was carried out one that was dead, the only son of his mother, and she was a widow: and much people of the city was with her. And he came nigh and touched the bier: and the bearers stood still. And he said, Young man, I say unto thee, Arise. And he that was dead sat up, and began to speak. And fear took hold on all: and they glorified God, saying, A great prophet is risen among us: and, God hath visited his people.

The story of the Gerasene demoniac is of interest not only for the problems associated with the action of Jesus in destroying a herd of swine and with the behaviour of the insane man, but also for the construction of the story which is skilfully dramatic. The scene changes from the place of healing to the mountain side by the lake, then to the city, then back to the place of healing. This is quite unusual in Miracle-Stories, and it has been reasonably held to be a bazaar-tale based on a historical cure of a demented person, and giving the popular belief concerning demons.

The number of pigs, " about 2,000 " is not mentioned in Matthew and Luke. There is no heightening of the miracle in this or other respects by these two evangelists.

THE HISTORICAL VALUE OF MIRACLE-STORIES

The existence of formal characteristics must necessarily raise the question of historical veracity. This has been doubted on various grounds. Dibelius finds in them a secular tone. The Novellen are not conditioned " by the thoughts found in the preaching of salvation." Rather they are dominated by the desire to show the nature of our Lord's intervention, and to proclaim the greatness of His miracles when human aid could give no relief. The coming of Jesus into the world to save mankind falls into the background. When Dibelius characterizes the narratives as " secular " he does not mean that the material itself is of non-Christian origin. " Yet there is a certain relationship of mind between the Gospel Tales and the non-Christian miracle-stories, and thus a certain approximation to the ' literature ' of the world, not, of course, to fine literature, but to popular literature and indeed to the writing of the people." The historical value of a Novelle depends on its origin, and there are three ways in which Novellen might arise. They are (1) the enlargement of a brief Paradigm narrative, giving rise to hybrid forms; (2) the filling out of a Paradigm by the insertion of a motive, as in the Walking on the Sea where a case of help given by Jesus in a storm was probably extended by the motif, " He wished to pass them by "; (3) the taking over and transformation of non-Christian stories as in the Gerasene Demoniac and the Wedding at Cana. " Historical foundations or commencements may be presupposed when a Paradigm is the basis of a Tale ; and only when a non-Christian story seems to be probable as the original of a Christian Tale is the reliability of the Christian narrative really brought into question " (p. 102). It may be inferred from this quotation that there are only two Miracle-Stories which have not at least an historical basis.

Dibelius is not affected in his judgment by the fact that the literary style of narrative with its three characteristics is common to popular Tales and to the Gospel Miracle-Stories. Not so Bultmann. He is very sceptical indeed. Miracle-Stories are of literary origin as may be seen in all ancient miracle-stories. But he makes one remarkable admission. Compared with Hellenistic stories, the New Testament Miracle-Stories in describing cures " are extremely reserved in this respect, since they hesitate to attribute to the person of Jesus the magical traits which were often characteristic of the Hellenistic miracle worker."

To these views must be added the theory that in them all Jesus is set forth as a thaumaturge, a wonderworker. Not only so. There is a religious motive in these secular tales. Jesus is represented as the Lord of divine powers. So says Dibelius. He adds that story-tellers have given indications of it in three stories where secrecy surrounds the action of Jesus. " The miracle worker avoids the public because He is an envoy and revealer of God, who does not allow his action, i.e., God's action, to be seen by profane eyes . . . The vision of God, however, is not granted to the majority " (p. 94). The three stories are the Raising of Jairus' Daughter, the Deaf Mute when Jesus withdraws him from the crowd, and the Blind Man when He leaves the village. From these three incidents Dibelius infers that the real object of other miracles was to prove an Epiphany of the divine on earth, as in the Tempest, the Feeding of the Five Thousand, the Walking on the Sea, and in the Epileptic Boy, where we read, " How long shall I be with you? How long shall I bear with you? "

Thus Dibelius, who agrees with other Form Critics that Jesus is represented as a worker of miracles, finds a deeper religious motive in some of the miracles.

Of the various issues raised by Form Criticism some are not new and others would arise in any Historical Criticism of the Gospel story, quite apart from the literary-historical method of Gospel study. The two important issues raised by Form Criticism are these. (1) Does the existence of stories with similar structural forms in non-Christian literature vitiate the truth of the Gospel Miracle-Stories? Bultmann says Yes. (2) Is the faith mentioned in the Gospel Stories a mechanical faith? Form Critics say Yes.

1. That the parallels exist is not open to doubt. Vincent Taylor has called attention to a most interesting parallel to the Widow's Son. It is told of Apollonius of Tyana :

A girl had died just in the hour of her marriage, and the bridegroom was following her bier lamenting as was natural his marriage left unfulfilled, and the whole of Rome was mourning with him, for the maiden belonged to a consular family. Apollonius then, witnessing their grief, said, " Put down the bier, for I will stay the tears that you are shedding for this maiden." And withal he asked what was her name. . . . Merely touching her and whispering in secret some spell over her, he at once woke up the maiden from her seeming death; and the girl spoke out loud and returned to her father's house, just as Alcestis when she was brought back to life by Hercules.

The parallels are to be found in each of the three elements of Miracle-Stories. Lucian reports the cure of many " who fell down in fits, rolled their eyes, and foamed at the mouth." Other stories record that a sick woman laughed scornfully when she heard of the healing powers of the God Asclepius or that a multitude laughed at the idea of blind men receiving sight. We read of similar happenings in the Gospels. We read also in the Gospels and in Greek tales of the use of spittle, of the use of words in a foreign tongue, and of the laying on of hands. But we do not read in the Gospels of Jesus, as Exorcist, holding a ring to the sufferer's nose, or of placing a piece of a virgin's gravestone on a poisoned foot, or of demons destroying statues. We may recall Bultmann's candid admission that the Gospel stories are more restrained and more reserved in the magical traits attributed to Jesus.

The obvious criticism to be made is that similarity of form is no evidence of truth or falsity. In fact, the structural forms are not necessarily artificial, but are obvious and natural in any story which does not make its climax a saying of Jesus. It is to be expected that a story of healing ending in a cure, would describe the initial circumstances such as the length and nature of the illness, the cure effected and the means, if any, and the effect of the cure. There is therefore nothing extraordinary in the existence of the parallelism in form between Gospel miracle-stories and non-Christian miracle-stories. What does come out of the comparison is the admission of Bultmann that the Gospel narratives are marked

I

by a sense of care and reserve.   Jesus, we may add, used just those methods and those means which were familiar in His days in order to win the patient's confidence and, through commonly accepted ideas, awaken the patient's faith in Him and in the possibility of a cure.   The Gospel narrative asserts that where faith was lacking, wondrous works could not be performed.

2. The mention of faith leads to another criticism of the views of Form Critics. They argue as if faith in these narratives is only faith in the ability of Jesus to do wonders, that the power of Jesus was displayed mechanically without any necessary response from those who received a boon, that in all cases it might be said that " virtue went out of Him."   We must inquire whether there is any truth in this theory and in particular whether evidence exists that Jesus, at least on occasions, expected a personal faith from those who asked His help.

That Jesus did heal without calling on human faith in Him is to be seen in the Gospels. Instances are to be found in the narratives of the Gerasene demoniac, in the wedding at Cana, and the Widow's Son, but not in all miracles. There is evidence that Jesus required and acknowledged human faith. In the cure of the man with leprosy, the leper says, " If thou wilt, thou canst make me clean," and this prayer, evidencing his faith, is offered up on his knees. Jesus, moved with compassion, responds by granting his request.   " I will; be thou clean." A second instance is in the story of the Epileptic Boy where the father, when Jesus says to him, " All things are possible to him that believeth," cries out " I believe; help thou mine unbelief."   A third instance is our Lord's words to Jairus, "Fear not, only believe."

The story of the Woman with the Issue of Blood calls for some examination. The woman evidently believed, with others in that age (Acts xix, 12) that a supernatural power was attached to the garments of saintly men. She therefore touched our Lord's garment. The faith of the woman was acknowledged by Jesus, "Daughter, thy faith hath made thee whole." Even if the words in the story that "Jesus perceived in himself that power had gone forth from him," are traditional, they are only found here and do not permit a general deduction that the power of Jesus acted mechanically in all cases. Mark, on the contrary, says, in the account of our Lord's visit to Nazareth, "And he could there do no mighty work, save that he laid his hands upon a few sick folk, and healed them. And he marvelled because of their unbelief" (vi, 5–6). In the Lucan account of the miracle, the narrative portion relating to the "virtue" in the garments is put into our Lord's mouth, "for I perceived that power had gone forth from me." Matthew omits all reference to the going forth of "virtue" and makes the cure one of faith on the woman's part.

Hence we may conclude that Jesus required this personal faith in Him and that it is a genuine part of the tradition. Now, in non-Christian tales such a demand is unknown ; in them the cures are magical. There exists therefore a vital difference between the Christian and non-Christian parallel Miracle-Stories. An element is to be found in the Christian stories, which is unique. Parallelism fails in the most important element.

That stories of cures in non-Christian literature may be true is not questioned. Jesus Himself said that the casting out of devils was done by others (Luke xi, 19 ; Mark ix, 38–40).

One problem still remains. Are the miracles true? Did they happen as they are recorded by Mark?

Had a modern scientific observer been present in those days we should doubtless have had such versions of the miracles as might have satisfied our thirst for information. Had there been more than one observer, it would not follow that their reports would have agreed in every detail, for much would depend on the unknown personal equation. Doubtless they would have agreed on the main facts. But still there would have been one difference of supreme importance, namely, their respective views of Jesus and their estimate of His personality. Would they have understood His plan of work? Would they have possessed the penetrative power possessed by those who "were with Him," who dwelt in His company, who were eye-witnesses of His majesty? Would they also have understood the outlook and the beliefs and the feelings of Eastern primitive sufferers, their ignorance of laws of nature and laws of health, their superstition, their childish fear of evil spirits, their conception of the delusions of the insane? We ask these questions because the Gospel narratives reflect the views of their age, and thereby bear the marks of veracity. The narratives are genuine to this extent that their environment is reliable.

Again, the modern scientific outlook is not as sceptical on the possibility of miracles as it was a

few decades before. Modern healings and modern
cures of mental patients have made a sympathetic
approach to the healing miracles of Jesus possible.
We recognize, as the evangelists did not, the distinction between organic and nervous disorders.
We understand the importance of the patient's faith
in the physician, the value of the surroundings,
the will to live. It is not the healing-miracles
which trouble men's minds to-day but the miracles
over nature. The late Dr. Burkitt wrote, " I
confess that I see no way to treat the Feeding of the
Five Thousand except by a process of frank rationalization. . . . The solution which alone appeals to
me is that Jesus told the disciples to distribute their
scanty store, and that their example made those
who were well provided share with those who had
little " (*Jesus Christ*, p. 32). Dr. Burkitt's opinion
cannot be neglected. He might be right. A
similar rationalization might explain the Walking on
the Sea and the Stilling of the Tempest.

But to the minds of the Evangelists there was no
distinction between the miracles. They did not
classify them and tabulate them. The miracles
were all " works " of Jesus. They are essentially
acts of One who was sympathetic with suffering and
yet came not primarily to heal and to display His
power over nature but to redeem mankind. To the
writer of the primary Gospel, Jesus went about
doing good, but the acts of goodness were not proofs
of His Messiahship. That was a later inference as
we see in the Fourth Gospel.

Thus in the records of Mark, miracles had no
evidential value. Jesus Himself did not regard
faith in miracles as necessary for human salvation.

He certainly did not claim to have a desire to be thought a thaumaturge. This view is held to-day by many Christian believers to whom miracles are not the proof of Divinity. We can believe in the Incarnate Lord without believing that He stilled the storm by a word or walked on the sea or fed a multitude with five small loaves and two fishes. We can believe in Jesus as Saviour and Redeemer without deciding whether the nature-miracles are true or not. We can leave the question open, because of our ignorance of what really happened. The historical truth of the miracles cannot be solved by Form Criticism or by Historical Criticism. It is essentially a problem of philosophy, if not of Christian philosophy. All we need to know is that the early Church believed that God had visited and redeemed His people.

Chapter V

SAYINGS AND PARABLES

A rough distinction may be drawn between the Sayings and Parables of the Gospels by confining the term Parables to the longer sayings where a comparison is made. This distinction is advisable, for whilst parables possess form, sayings are " formless," that is to say, the Sayings cannot be divided into groups possessing popular forms. Sayings can only be differentiated according to their poetical structure or their contents.

We have already seen that sayings circulated not only independently but also in larger units, and that these larger units might with reason be attributed to the genius of Jesus, who, as a Rabbi, put them into various kinds of parallelism and rhythm in order that they might be easily learnt and remembered (see pp. 42 ff.). We have also seen that Apothegm-Stories were valued for the saying or pronouncement which was set in a narrative framework. Lastly we had occasion to draw attention to Bultmann's contention that whilst the narrative portions of the Apothegms were untrustworthy, the sayings in them might be authentic and that he therefore sought for some clues from the independent sayings which might be indications of historical truth (see pp. 31 f.).

Let us deal first with the Sayings of our Lord. We shall here not consider those which form the kernel of Apothegm-Stories, nor the Parables to which we shall give attention later.

THE SAYINGS OF OUR LORD

It will probably simplify our study of the Sayings if we considered them under three headings. First, Bultmann's classification and his conclusions therefrom. Secondly, the importance attached to the pronouncements of Jesus in the primitive Church. This will be evidence of the genuineness of at least the greater part of the traditional sayings. Thirdly, the causes which might have affected sayings during transmission.

Bultmann's classification. The Sayings are arranged in five groups.

1. Logia which are words of wisdom of the type found in the *Proverbs of Solomon* and in *Ecclesiasticus* or the *Wisdom of Jesus the Son of Sirach.* The majority of our Lord's sayings have parallels in Jewish Wisdom literature, and so many are the analogies that no ethical precept of Jesus need be entirely unique. It is possible that Jesus originated some of the Gospel Logia but it is also possible that many Jewish proverbs were placed in His mouth by the primitive Church. " The Wisdom-sayings or Logia are least guaranteed to be authentic words of Jesus."

2. *Prophetic and Apocalyptic Sayings* in which Jesus proclaimed the coming of the Reign of God and gave a call to repentance. The eschatological enthusiasm of the early Church was due to the appearance of Jesus as a prophet. Sayings therefore of this particular kind such as Matt. v, 39b–41 ; v, 44–48 ; xi, 5–6 ; Mark iii, 27 ; vii, 15 ; viii, 35; Luke vi, 20 f.; x, 23, include original utterances of a prophetic personality. But authentic sayings of Jesus were supplemented by the prophets of the

early Church, and probably some of their own utterances were attributed to Jesus. These latter include
those relating to the Church in Matt. xvi, 18–19
and xxviii, 19–20.

3. *Law-words and Community-Rules.* In this
group, sayings of Jesus on purity (Mark vii, 15),
divorce (Mark x, 11–12) and on almsgiving, prayer
and fasting go back to the personality of Jesus.
But the sayings which contain rules for discipline
and for the mission of the Church are doubtfully
attributed to Jesus. For example Matt. xviii, 15–
22 ; x, 5–16 ; Mark vii, 20–23 ; Luke xxi, 34–36 ;
the Passion-predictions of Mark (viii, 31 ; ix, 31 ;
x, 33–34), and the saying of Mark x, 45, were
created by the Christian community. In fact, " the
sayings in which the Church expressed its faith in
Jesus, His work, His destiny and His Person " are
community creations.

4. " *I* " *words*, or sayings in the first person
singular. Only a very few authentic. Most of
them involve the Messianic consciousness.

5. *Parables.*
Bultmann's conclusion had best be given in his
own words. " Though one may admit the fact
that for no single word of Jesus is it possible to
produce positive evidence of its authenticity, still
one may point to a whole series of words found in
the oldest stratum of tradition which do give us a
consistent representation of the historical message
of Jesus " (p. 61). These authentic sayings include the following from Mark.

Can the sons of the bride-chamber fast, while the bridegroom is with them ? (ii, 19a).

Is it lawful on the sabbath day to do good, or to do harm? to save a life, or to kill? (iii, 4).

No one can enter into the house of the strong man, and spoil his goods, except he first bind the strong man; and then he will spoil his house (iii, 27).

There is nothing from without the man, that going into him can defile him: but the things which proceed out of the man are those that defile the man (vii, 15).

Whosoever would save his life shall lose it; and whosoever shall lose his life (for my sake and the gospel's) shall save it (viii, 35).

Whosoever shall be ashamed of me and of my words in this adulterous and sinful generation, the Son of man also shall be ashamed of him, when he cometh in the glory of his Father with the holy angels (viii, 38).

Whosoever shall put away his wife, and marry another, committeth adultery against her: and if she herself shall put away her husband, and marry another, she committeth adultery (x, 11–12).

Whosoever shall not receive the kingdom of God as a little child, he shall in no wise enter therein (x, 15).

The following passages in Luke are allowed to stand as genuine utterances of Jesus.

Blessed are ye poor: for yours is the kingdom of God. Blessed are ye that hunger now: for ye shall be filled. Blessed are ye that weep now: for ye shall laugh (vi, 20–21).

Why call ye me, Lord, Lord, and do not the things which I say? (vi, 46).

Leave the dead to bury their own dead; but go thou and publish abroad the kingdom of God (ix, 60).

No man, having put his hand to the plough, and looking back, is fit for the kingdom of God (ix, 62).

Blessed are the eyes which see the things that ye see: for I say unto you, that many prophets and kings desired to see the things which ye see, and saw them not; and to hear the things which ye hear, and heard them not (x, 23–24).

When ye see a cloud rising in the west, straightway ye say, There cometh a shower; and so it cometh to pass. And when ye see a south wind blowing, ye say, There will be a scorching heat; and it cometh to pass. Ye hypocrites, ye know how to interpret the face of the earth and the heaven; but how is that ye know not how to interpret this time? (xii, 54–56).

If any man cometh unto me, and hateth not his own father, and mother, and wife, and children, and brethren, and sisters, yea, and his own life also, he cannot be my disciple. Whosoever doth not bear his own cross and come after me, cannot be my disciple (xiv, 26–27).

From Matthew, Bultmann accepts the following amongst the trustworthy sayings:

Ye have heard that it was said to them of old time, Thou shalt not kill; and whosoever shall kill shall be in danger of the judgment: but I say unto you, that everyone who is angry with his brother shall be in danger of the judgment; and whosoever shall say to his brother, Raca, shall be in danger of the council; and whosoever shall say, Thou fool, shall be in danger of the hell of fire (v, 21–22).

Ye have heard that it was said, Thou shalt not commit adultery: but I say unto you, that everyone that looketh on a woman to lust after her hath committed adultery with her already in his heart (v, 27–28).

Ye have heard that it was said to them of old time, Thou shalt not forswear thyself, but shalt perform unto the Lord thine oaths: but I say unto you, Swear not at all; neither by the heaven, for it is the throne of God; nor by the earth, for it is the footstool of his feet; nor by Jerusalem, for it is the city of the great King. Neither shalt thou swear by thy head, for thou canst not make one hair white or black. But let your speech be, Yea, yea; Nay, nay: and whatsoever is more than these is of the evil one (v, 33–37).

Whosoever smiteth thee on thy right cheek, turn to him the other also.   And if any man would go to law with thee, and take away thy coat, let him have thy cloke also.   And whosoever shall compel thee to go one mile, go with him twain (v, 39b–41).

Love your enemies, and pray for them that persecute you; that ye may be sons of your Father which is in heaven: for he maketh his sun to rise on the evil and the good, and sendeth rain on the just and the unjust.   For if ye love them that love you, what reward have ye? do not even the publicans the same?   And if ye salute your brethren only, what do ye more than others? do not even the Gentiles the same?   Ye therefore shall be perfect, as your heavenly Father is perfect (v, 44–48).

When therefore thou doest alms . . . And when ye pray . . . Moreover when ye fast . . . (vi, 2–18).

Enter ye in by the narrow gate: for wide is the gate, and broad is the way, that leadeth to destruction, and many be they that enter in thereby.   For narrow is the gate, and straitened the way, that leadeth unto life, and few be they that find it (vii, 13–14).

The blind receive their sight, and the lame walk, the lepers are cleansed, and the deaf hear, and the dead are raised up, and the poor have good tidings preached to them.   And blessed is he, whosoever shall find none occasion of stumbling in me (xi, 5–6).

But if I by the spirit of God cast out devils, then is the kingdom of God come upon you (xii, 28).

Woe unto ye, ye blind guides . . . Woe unto you, scribes and Pharisees, hypocrites . . . (xxiii, 16–19, 23–26).

It is remarkable that Bultmann admits as authentic our Lord's words on His miracles (Matt. xi, 5–6; xii, 28).   And yet the critic pronounces that the miracles of Jesus are untrustworthy.

The sayings which Bultmann accepts are chiefly

eschatological and ethical.   He is concerned about
the relation between our Lord's eschatological and
ethical teaching, and the two schools of thought
represented by Wellhausen (ethical) and Schweitzer
(eschatological).   By the methods of Form Criticism
he discovers he has found room for both.   " Christ's
demands have an absolute character . . . . He taught
men that the present instant is the moment of
decision, in which it is possible to yield up every
claim of one's own and submit obediently to the
will of God.   It is this way of the good will, that
Jesus preached, which leads man directly to the
awareness of his own unworthiness and worthless-
ness in the sight of God, and of his own situation as
faced with inevitable decision ; it is only here that he
learns the profoundest meaning of God's forgiveness,
which one can receive only as a little child " (pp.
72 f.).

We are grateful to Bultmann for the words
we have just quoted.   But Jesus was more than a
teacher of ethics.   The early Church treasured
His teaching for deeper reasons than that it served
to guide conduct and morals.   It treasured our
Lord's words because they were His words, whereas
Bultmann's argument does not take sufficient account
of the personality of Jesus.   The critic in his search
for objective truth is too subjective and too heavily
biassed in favour of the creative power of the community.   The result is that the literary and rabbinical skill of the community is set against that of Jesus,
and, whilst every consideration in favour of the
community is stressed, the arguments in favour of
the creative power of a single personality like Jesus
hardly receive consideration.   The Church, says

Bultmann, made collections of popular logia for
purposes of teaching, including in them some forty
and no more authentic words of Jesus, and even
brought in secular proverbs and attributed them to
Jesus.

The Words of Jesus in the Church.   In view of
Bultmann's contention it will be necessary to turn to
such evidence as we can gain from the New Testament in regard to the preservation of sayings of
Jesus and the importance or otherwise of His sayings.
This inquiry is not the same as the attempt to
reconstruct Q, for we need here not the contents of
Q but authority for presuming that Q might be
authentic, irrespective of its contents.

We turn first to Mark.   Form Critics may raise
objections to the Marcan framework as genuine
records of the events of our Lord's ministry, but the
editorial redactions of the Evangelist are at least
good evidence of the beliefs of the age in which
Mark lived.   This is a reasonable inference from
the reiterated insistence of Form Critics that the
primitive Church was responsible for the texts of a
good proportion of the Gospel material.   In other
words, if an editorial statement is to be found in
Mark, we must immediately ask whether it was
" created by the community " or represented what
was accepted by the community and perhaps authen-
ticated by the community.   And further, if the redactional verses do not refer to the ministry of
Jesus but to conditions appertaining to the days of
the primitive Church, we must form some estimate
of the extent of such alteration or adaptation and
ask why this was done.   What then does Mark say
of collections of our Lord's sayings?   Were such

collections "created" or accepted as authentic?

In Mark we read, "And again he began to teach by the sea side. . . . And he taught them many things in parables." This statement is followed by the Parable of the Sower. Later, the explanation of this parable, which, by many scholars who are not Form Critics, is held to be a production of the Church, is preceded by the words, "And when he was alone, they that were round about him with the twelve asked of him the parables," and also by the phrases, "Know ye not this parable? And how shall ye know all the parables" (iv, 1, 2, 10, 13). This indicates that it was known in the early Church that there were other parables than that of the Sower, that Mark was giving only a selection. The evangelist makes a similar remark preceding the Parable of the Vineyard. "And he began to speak unto them in parables" (xii, 1).

Mark says much the same about sayings. Frequent are the references to teaching given by Jesus. "He entered into the synagogue and taught. And they were astonished at his teaching: for he taught them as having authority, and not as the scribes" (i, 21–22). "All the multitude resorted unto him, and he taught them" (ii, 13). Before the Feeding of the Five Thousand, "He began to teach them many things." When Jesus came into the borders of Judaea, "as he was wont, he taught them again" (x, 1). Mark does not give the contents of the teaching in these cases but implies that Jesus did teach and that it was thus believed in Marcan days. In two instances Mark does give specimens of the teaching. "And he called them unto him, and said unto them in parables, How can

Satan cast out Satan . . . No one can enter into the house of the strong man. . . . All their sins shall be forgiven unto the sons of men . . ." (iii, 22–30). We expect from the opening phrase, " in parables " much more than two or three metaphors and sayings. Again a hint of many sayings is implied in the passage which begins with " In his teaching he said," and continues with one warning against the scribes. We can from these references conclude that Mark knew more of " the teaching " than he gave in his Gospel.

Paul gives more definite evidence on this subject. To him the words of Jesus are final and his statements imply the existence of some authoritative written source from which he could quote. The positive statements of the words of Jesus in 1 Cor. vii, 10; ix, 14, are followed by another which reads as if the Apostle had consulted his written authority but could find no reference to the matter raised. " Now concerning virgins I have no commandment of the Lord: but I give my judgment " (1 Cor. vii, 25). Mention might be made of the request in one of the Pastoral Epistles, " The cloke that I left at Troas with Carpus, bring when thou comest, and the books, especially the parchments " (2 Timothy iv, 13). This evidence is invaluable if the argument of P. N. Harrison holds that iv, 13–15, is a genuine note made by Paul.[1] There were written records owned by and considered valuable by the Apostle. Was it from such a collection that he quoted the saying of the Lord Jesus which the elders of the Church at Ephesus were to remember, " It is more blessed to give

[1] *The Problem of the Pastoral Epistles.*

than to receive " (Acts xx, 35)? The saying is not found in the Gospel according to St. Luke, the companion of the Apostle, or in any of the Gospels. The practical necessity of remembering the words of our Lord Jesus was taught in the first century (1 Clem. xlvi, 8).

We quoted a passage of Dibelius in an earlier chapter on the existence of collections of sayings (see p. 35). He does not agree with Bultmann either about the date or the authenticity of Q. Dibelius is content to say that words of Jesus were already collected in the time of Paul and that Q gives a rough idea of such a collection.

We may now give Dibelius' solution of the relatively small quantity of sayings-tradition in Mark. " If we begin by noting that Mark obviously did not intend to write down the words of Jesus in their totality, we must see that this was not on account of personal prejudice, but because this tradition of the actual words had been preserved, in a way quite its own, separated from the handing down of general events, and kept for quite special purposes. . . . The fact that Mark does not give the material which we find in the Q sections of Matthew and Luke is not at all strange " (p. 260).

Thus we may safely say that Bultmann's view that only about forty sayings of Christ are historical is wrong. We must next examine the question whether sayings might have been altered in transmission and whether the early Church did so for any special reason.

THE SAYINGS AND THEIR TRANSMISSION

Instances occur in the Gospels where the sense of

K

the passages varies with the context and shows that the primitive community re-interpreted a saying to meet a new situation. In Mark x, 11–12, divorce is radically forbidden but in Matthew an exception is made. "Whosoever shall put away his wife, except for fornication, and shall marry another, committeth adultery" (xix, 9). It would seem that the Church modified the original saying of Jesus to meet the new conditions which arose from the delay of the Parousia. A similar tendency for the Church to plan out a rule of life free from eschatological expectations can be seen in the advice given to agree with one's adversary. The passage in Q, according to the Lucan text, reads as follows :

As thou art going with thine adversary before the magistrate, on the way give diligence to be quit of him ; lest haply he hale thee unto the judge, and the judge shall deliver thee to the officer, and the officer shall cast thee into prison. I say unto thee, Thou shalt by no means come out thence, till thou hast paid the very last mite (Luke xii, 58–59).

The context in Luke is eschatological. It was advisable to take precautions at once and not to wait for the coming judgment of the Messiah. This sense is clearly brought out in the context, for preceding the saying come references to discerning the signs of the times. The hearer is advised to settle his dispute without delay in face of a crisis. In Matthew v, 25 f., which was later than Q, there is no such reference to the Parousia.

There, the passage occurs in the Sermon on the Mount in the explanation attached to the commandment, "Thou shalt not kill." The old interpretation of the law must give place to the new as set forth by Jesus. Man must not be angry and should seek to be reconciled with a wrongdoer. If this brother has brought a law-suit against you, be sensible and make terms with him. Thus in Matthew there is no eschatological setting, and the passage has become a wise maxim for Christians. An admonition to reconciliation has replaced an earlier eschatological warning.

The sayings on savourless salt are instructive, and they appear in the three synoptic gospels. In Mark there is no interpretation and no context (see p. 41).

Salt is good: but if the salt have lost its saltness, wherewith will ye season it? Have salt in yourselves, and be at peace one with another (ix, 50).

Mark's meaning is not clear, except that he is referring to some Christian characteristic which one should possess. In Matthew, on the other hand, it means not a quality but the Christians themselves who are to be purifying agents.

Ye are the salt of the earth: but if the salt have lost its savour, wherewith shall it be salted? It is thenceforth good for nothing, but to be cast out and trodden under foot of men (v, 13).

Luke has a context of his own and it is distinct from that of Matthew and Mark. The reference to salt in Luke is found in a section which begins with the stringent requirements Jesus makes on those who would be His disciples. It involves hating members of one's family, taking up his cross and counting the cost.

So therefore whosoever he be of you that renounceth not all that he hath, he cannot be my disciple. Salt therefore is good: but if even the salt have lost its savour, wherewith shall it be seasoned ?   It is fit neither for the land nor for the dunghill ; men cast it out (xiv, 33–35).

Luke therefore interprets savourless salt as those who do not possess the courage to give up everything to follow Jesus.

It is clear that the meaning attached to the original saying on salt had been lost and that the evangelists therefore felt themselves at liberty to give a suitable meaning to it.   On the other hand the possibility cannot be overlooked that Jesus might have used the parabolic comparison in the Lucan sense, and that Matthew rightly applied it to Christians who had made the renunciation and should therefore be a purifying power in the world.   Matthew and Luke apply the metaphor in a personal sense.   The saying in Mark however is other than personal and is one of a series of independent sayings arranged for mnemonic purposes.

One other illustration will suffice.   The saying on darkness in Luke follows a warning against hypocrisy. The truth cannot be concealed and the disciples can be reassured that their words will be made known publicly however quietly they had first spoken them.

Whatsoever ye have said in the darkness shall be heard in the light ; and what ye have spoken in the ear in the inner chambers shall be proclaimed upon the housetops (xii, 3).

In Matthew, however, the saying is altered to give another meaning.   He places it in the Mission Charge to the Twelve and there it is a duty laid on the Apostles to proclaim the message delivered by Jesus to them.

What I tell you in the darkness, speak ye in the light ;

and what ye hear in the ear, proclaim upon the housetops (x, 27).

Thus sayings of Jesus were re-interpreted by the Church either to meet new conditions or because their original meaning had been lost. Also at times no indication is given in the Gospels of the occasion on which the words were spoken. But this does not mean that in the majority of such instances the original meaning cannot be recovered or that the majority of the sayings is to be traced to the community. For example we may take the saying on Savourless Salt. Dr. Dodd by taking the saying out of its context points out that it suggests a valuable commodity gone to waste by losing the one property which gives it value. In our Lord's own ministry such a tragedy was the state of Judaism in His time. " The *tertium comparationis* is simply the lamentable fact of a good and necessary thing irrevocably spoiled and wasted " (pp. 139–142).

Dibelius makes a very apposite remark on this matter. " The Christians believed themselves to be more faithful to their Master when they explained His sayings by expanding them, and then followed them with understanding, than if they had abhorred any addition and passed on the original form of His words." (*Fresh Approach to the New Testament*.)

PARABLES

Parables are sayings of various lengths in each of which a spiritual or moral truth is clearly enforced by means of a concrete analogy or comparison either expressed or implied.

The implications of this definition will be discussed presently, but before this is done one of the assumptions of Form Criticism must be considered. Did parables circulate singly or in collections? Two well-known collections are to be found in Mark and Matthew respectively, and we have seen that parabolic sayings exist in small collections mnemonically arranged. The groups in Mark and Matthew will serve as an introduction to the question.

The parables in Mark iv are the Sower, the Lamp under the Bushel, the Measure, the Seed Growing Secretly and the Mustard Seed. Of these the two last begin with an expressed comparison. " So is the kingdom of God, as if a man should cast seed upon the earth " (iv, 26). " How shall we liken the kingdom of God? or in what parable shall we set it forth? It is like a grain of mustard seed " (iv, 30 f.). Probably then the Seed Growing Secretly and the Mustard Seed formed a pair in oral tradition.

In Matthew xiii, we find the Sower, the Wheat and the Tares, the Mustard Seed, the Leaven, the Treasure in the Field, the Pearl of Great Price, the Drag-net. All but the Sower begin with the phrase, " The kingdom of Heaven is like unto." Of these six which begin thus, the Mustard Seed and the Leaven are separated from the rest by the explanation of the Wheat and the Tares. Probably the Treasure and the Pearl of Great Price circulated as a pair for they contain a common theme, namely that of sacrifice. The Drag-net and the Wheat and the Tares which are separated both end with eschatological teaching. Matthew evidently added parables from Q and his special source (M) to the three he obtained from Mark.

Now in Mark, the Mustard Seed is joined with the Seed growing Secretly, whereas in Matthew it is

joined with the Leaven. Luke has the same
grouping as in Matthew (Luke xiii, 18–21). It is
therefore not easy to decide which of them might
have formed a pair in oral tradition; and this
further affects the interpretation of the Leaven for
the interpretation depends on its association with the
Mustard Seed or its independence as a unit. All we
can infer is that the Mustard Seed probably formed
one of a pair.

Thus we are left so far with the Treasure in the
Field and the Pearl of Great Price as a combination
in the formative period. We find another certain
pair in the Patched Garment and the Wineskins
(Mark ii, 21–22). Another pair is given by Luke—
the Building of the Tower, and the King at War
(xiv, 28–33).

In Luke there is the trilogy of parables, the Lost
Sheep, the Lost Coin and the Prodigal Son (Luke
xv). Of these the Lost Sheep is found in a different
context in Matthew (xviii, 12–14). Probably the
Lucan pair, the Lost Sheep and the Lost Coin,
circulated together for their treatment is alike; they
are short, and contain words which are wanting in
the Prodigal Son—about the joy in heaven or
amongst the angels of God over one sinner that
repenteth.

The Waiting Servants, the Thief at Night and
the Master and Servant are given together in Luke
(xii, 36–38, 39–40, 43–48). The latter two are
also found in Matthew (xxiv, 43–44, 45–51), but
whether any two of them—one being the Thief at
Night—formed a pair is uncertain. It is probable
that the three existed as a trilogy in Q, though the
Waiting Servants is peculiar to Luke.

In the oral period therefore a few parables circulated originally in pairs, and Mark and Matthew
grouped them according to theme.

Many of the Parables contain introductions
which are editorial, e.g., " He spake unto them in
parables." An elaborate introduction inserted by
Luke, who thereby altered the original meaning of
the parable, is that prefixed to the Pounds. " And
as they heard these things, he added and spake a
parable, because he was nigh to Jerusalem, and
because they supposed that the kingdom of God was
immediately to appear " (xix, 11).

THE FORMAL CHARACTERISTICS OF PARABLES

Of the sayings of Jesus, the only group which
possesses form is that of Parables. We saw that
all other sayings, such as Logia or Apocalyptic-words
or I-words or Law-words, possess no form whatever
and are simply classifications based on the nature of
their contents.

The definition of parables given above is meant to
include the distinctive features of parables, which are
four in number and may include a fifth.

1. First, there must be a comparison, expressed
or implied. When expressed, words are used of the
type, " like " " even as " " as." When implied,
the saying may be metaphorical, e.g. " Cast not your
pearls before swine " ; " Ye are the salt of the earth " ;
" Can the blind lead the blind ? " This comparison
will be found whatever the nature of the parables
may be, that is whether they are metaphors, en-
larged metaphors, similitudes, illustrative examples,
and so on.

This comparison may run through a long story

complete in itself, to which the title Novellen might be given, e.g., the Prodigal Son, the Unforgiving Servant, the Pounds. However, it is the group called the Similitudes that is of interest. This group includes sayings such as the Beam and the Mote, the Fig-tree Withered, the Patched Garment, the Children of the Bride Chamber, the Children in the Market Place—all parables which contain words such as " like," " even as," or " as." It is these Similitudes which give all the characteristics of parables in the highest degree.

2. The second characteristic is that the comparison must be simple. The aim of the parable is not to conceal but to teach a simple lesson clearly. The illustration must be a fact of experience, real or imaginary, and not involved. In point of fact, all our Lord's illustrations are drawn from the ordinary happenings of nature or of social life. If the illustration is unusual, as in the equal payment of the men who worked unequal hours in the vineyard, or in the millions of pounds owed by the unforgiving servant, or in the huge beam in the eye, the purpose is to excite interest by the eccentricity. In all cases the experience would be appreciated by all hearers and would convey the spiritual truth. Many of the illustrations may have been drawn from actual historical happenings known to Jesus, such as the prodigal son, the coin lost by the woman, the lost sheep, the king at war, the two sons, the sower, the wheat and the tares, the splinter in the eye, the lamp in the house. It is even possible that, as Shakespeare did in later centuries, Jesus utilized events taken from current stories or adapted parabolic sayings from Rabbinical sources, but He proved

Himself a greater than either a Shakespeare or a Solomon. Dodd has well said in his book on the Parables, " The Kingdom of God is intrinsically like the processes of nature and of the daily life of men." Jesus found the spiritual order exemplified in the facts of nature, and " this sense of the divineness of the natural order is the major premiss of all the parables " (p. 22).

3. The third distinctive characteristic of the parables is that each should possess one application and only one. The comparison should not extend to details ; that is, the parable should not be turned into an allegory unless it was so framed by Jesus and formed an intrinsic and integral part of the parable. This is definitely the case in the Wicked Husbandmen, but even in this parable Jesus did not explain the allegory. This single application is the *tertium comparationis*. Forgetfulness of this principle has commonly led to a wrong exegesis however homiletically possible the parable might be. A few illustrations will make this clear.

In the Treasure in the Field the man who discovered the treasure acts in a morally doubtful manner. He hides the treasure and buys the field cheaply, it would seem at the market price. The Unjust Steward is guilty of unscrupulous conduct in deceiving his master. Jesus did not mean these details to be stressed, for that would mean turning the parables into allegories. The wrongful conduct of the men is not to be copied. The emphasis, the *tertium comparationis*, in the Hidden Treasure is the willingness of the finder to make every sacrifice at a critical time to gain something of known inestimable value, and in the Unjust Steward the necessity of making a decision and acting decisively at a crisis.

The principle that parables should not be turned into allegories can be easily illustrated. Take that of the unexpected guest at midnight.

Which of you shall have a friend, and shall go unto him at midnight, and say to him, Friend, lend me three loaves; for a friend of mine is come to me from a journey, and I have nothing to set before him; and he from within shall answer and say, Trouble me not: the door is now shut, and my children are with me in bed; I cannot rise and give thee? I say unto you, Though he will not rise and give him, because he is his friend, yet because of his importunity he will arise and give him as many as he needeth (Luke xi, 5–8).

Even homiletically, an attempt to find who is represented by the unexpected visitor or the children in bed, and to identify the man in bed with God is ridiculous. The one application of the parable is that when a critical situation arises—and here it comes at an awkward and untimely hour—action must be taken to meet the situation. The moral is in the story itself. This parable comes from Luke, who gives four other parables of the same kind. These have been called Illustrative Stories by Julicher who however only applies the term to the other four—the Good Samaritan (x, 30–37), the Rich Fool (xii, 16–20), the Rich Man and Lazarus (xvi, 19–31), and the Pharisee and the Publican (xviii, 9–14). The lesson, which is ethical, is in the story itself and the hearers would make the application by inference.

If then Jesus did not mean parables to be treated as allegories, how comes it that Jesus is said to have given allegorical explanations to the Sower and the Tares in Mark, and also in two instances in John, the Door and the Sheepfold, and the Vine and the Branches? Did He not give an allegory in the Wicked Husbandman, and insert an allegory of the King at War with rebels in the Talents? The answer to these questions depends first on the statement of Mark iv, 10–12, 33–34, between which is the explanation of the Sower. Did Jesus make the statement and give the explanation?

Mark iv, 11–12, 33–34. And he said unto them (the twelve) Unto you is given the mystery of the kingdom of God: but unto them that are without, all things are done in parables: that seeing they may see, and not perceive; and hearing they may hear, and not understand; lest haply they should turn again, and it should be forgiven them.

Later in verses 33 and 34 we get the evangelist's own comments.

And with many such parables spake he the word unto them, as they were able to hear it: and without a parable spake he not unto them: but privately to his own disciples he expounded all things.

The difficulties in attributing the statement in verses 11–12 to Jesus are as follows (1) As they stand, the obvious meaning is that Jesus meant His parables to conceal truth, and that by them He intended to harden men's hearts so that they should not understand the parables. But this is so contrary to the character of Jesus that it cannot be accepted. Further, it stultifies the very purpose of parables which were intentionally directed to reaching the hardened hearer. This purpose is admitted by Mark, who in spite of the statement in iv, 11–12, gives the parable of the Vineyard and adds at the end, "and they sought to lay hold on him; and they feared the multitude; for they perceived that he spake the parable against them: and they left him, and went away" (xii, 12). The opponents of Jesus saw, perceived, and understood the parable. And in Mark iv, 13, Jesus seems surprised that the disciples could not understand His parable of the Sower. In other words, the parable was not so obscure that it could not have been understood—a direct contradiction of the statement attributed to Jesus in the two preceding verses. (2) Again, in the early Church, there was a tendency to identify speaking "in the spirit" with words of Jesus (Acts xi, 28; xvi, 6). Mark iv, 10–12, may be an illustration of this tendency. A scriptural quotation which explained a problem of the primitive Church could be attributed to Jesus because it was scriptural. The problem is that raised and discussed by Paul in Romans ix, 1. "Did God cast off His people? God forbid." They were hardened. "God gave them a spirit of stupor, eyes that they should not see, and ears that they should not hear unto this very day" (xi, 7–8). The multitude of Hebrews did not accept Jesus as Messiah because God had so willed it. It is clear that the idea of a judicial hardening was a doctrine of the early Church and it is applied here to teaching by parables.

In other words, the attribution of the statement to Jesus in Mark iv, 10–12 is the evangelist's own contribution, and the view there expressed was the view of the Church to explain why the large majority of Jews was unresponsive. Further support is given by the vocabulary, e.g., the word "mystery" is found nowhere else in the synoptic gospels; neither is "they that are without," which may be contrasted with "they that are of the Way."

Turning to the Parable of the Sower itself, the discrepancy in the treatment is obvious. In the allegorical explanation whilst the seed is the Word, that which comes from the seed is different groups of people. Again the interest in the parable is in the Sower, in the explanation it is in the different kinds of soil. For this and other reasons it has been held that the explanation of the Parable is in reality an early sermon on it. The explanation of the Sower, which is allegorical in character, was the work of the early Church. So also it may have been with the explanation of the Wheat and the Tares where the allegory is wholly eschatological.

4. The fourth characteristic of parables is that they are meant to win assent for a spiritual truth. The hearers are expected to make a decision. " Can the sons of the bridegroom fast, while the bridegroom is with them? " " What thinkest thou? " (Matt. xvii, 25). " How think ye? " (Matt. xviii, 12). " What thinketh ye? " (Matt. xxi, 28). So also the hearers are called upon to express their judgment when, for example, Jesus spoke of the Good Samaritan, the Pharisee and Publican, the Hidden Treasure and so on. Did not the Samaritan act rightly? Was not the Publican justified? Was the man who purchased the field to buy the treasure wise?

It is possible that in the Unjust Steward, the difficult passage about commending the steward should read " Did the Lord commend the unrighteous steward because he had done wisely? " (Luke xvi, 8). We have a similar question in the Vineyard parable. " What therefore will the lord of the vineyard do? " (Mark xii, 9).

A probable fifth characteristic was mentioned. I owe this to Dr. Dodd's book referred to, and the characteristic, if accepted, would read as follows. The application must bear upon the ministry of Jesus, which was the coming of the kingdom. The parables represent our Lord's interpretation of His ministry.

This implies two things. The *Sitz im Leben* was actually the situation in which Christ was. It was not the eschatological situation of the early Church. The Parables thus show the creative genius of Jesus, and were not creations of the community.

Dodd proceeds therefore to attempt a reconstruction in order to find the original life-situation. Certain parables show this situation clearly such as the Hidden Treasure and the Pearl, the Lost Sheep, the Lost Coin, the Prodigal Son, the Great Feast, the Wicked Husbandman, etc. Of the other Parables, some refer to a crisis, namely, the Waiting Servants, the Faithful and Unfaithful Servants, the Thief at Night, the Ten Virgins. Of these parables of crisis Dodd says, " They were intended to enforce His appeal to men to recognize that the Kingdom of God was present in all its momentous consequences, and that by their conduct in the presence of this tremendous crisis they would judge themselves as faithful or unfaithful, wise or foolish. When the crisis had passed, they were adapted by the Church to enforce its appeal to men to prepare for the second and final world-crisis which it believed to be approaching " (p. 174). Of the Parables of Growth namely, the Sower, the Tares, the Seed Growing Secretly, the Mustard Seed, the Leaven and the

Drag-net, Dodd writes, " They are not to be taken as implying a long process of ·development introduced by the ministry of Jesus and to be consummated by His second advent, though the Church later understood them in that sense.   As in the teaching of Jesus as a whole so here, there is no long historical perspective ; the *eschaton*, the divinely ordained climax of history, is here.   It has come by no human effort, but by act of God ; and yet not by an arbitrary, catastrophic intervention, for it is the harvest following upon a process of growth " (p. 193).   Dodd has given a positive construction of the views of Dibelius that the sayings of Jesus were originally gathered together for a hortatory end, and that there was a tendency of the Churches to derive as much exhortation as possible from the words of Jesus (pp. 246, 257).

Chapter VI

THE PASSION NARRATIVE

Form Critics agree that a Passion Story was the first narrative to be written down and that it was written early in the formative period. It was a continuous story, and its probable contents can be discovered with some assurance. Thus while many of the Apothegm-Stories, Miracle-Stories, Sayings and Parables, and stories of Jesus circulated as self-detached units in the early days of the Church, the Passion Story was an exception.

The evidence for this is in the New Testament. The Passion was a fixed part of the preaching in Apostolic days, and the narration of it was necessary because the whole gospel of salvation depended on it (see pp. 64 ff.). Again, the four Evangelists devote the greater part of the contents of the Gospels to the details of the Passion. It has even been claimed that those sections of the Gospels which precede the Passion story were meant to be introductions to it. Further, in the four Gospels the agreement between them is remarkable. Even John, who departs from the other Evangelists in detail, agrees with the main facts of the Passion and in the order in which they occurred. Lastly the life-situation of the Church demanded a continuous story to prove, particularly by an appeal to scripture, that it was necessary that the Messiah should die, that His death was in accordance with the will of God, and that by His death and resurrection He proved He was the Saviour of mankind.

" The Passion Story," says Dibelius, " is the only piece of Gospel tradition which in early times gave events in their larger connection " (p. 179). The sceptical Bultmann agrees that " it was the death and resurrection of Jesus, viewed as a unity, which was the decisive event in the progress of salvation " and that " it is quite conceivable that a continuous account of the events of the Passion Narrative would be handed down at a very early period " (p. 64 f.).

A number of questions arise immediately. Are there any independent units in the Passion Narratives which were first handed down in isolation and were later attached to the main accounts? What were the contents of the primitive narratives? How many distinct Passion narratives may be traced in the Gospels? What is the significance of the frequent references to scripture which are made in the Gospel narratives?

Independent Units. The story of the Anointing is clearly a self-detached unit, and was inserted into the main narrative because of its reference to the burial. " She hath done what she could : she hath anointed my body aforehand for the burying " (Mark xiv, 3–9). Further, the removal of this incident from Mark makes the evangelist's narrative read as a consecutive order of events.

Now after two days was the feast of the passover and the unleavened bread : and the chief priests and the scribes sought how they might take him with subtilty, and kill him : for they said, Not during the feast, lest haply there shall be a tumult of the people (xiv, 1–2).

And Judas Iscariot, he that was one of the twelve, went away unto the chief priests, that he might deliver him unto them. And they, when they heard it, were glad, and promised to give him money. And he sought how he might conveniently deliver him unto them (xiv, 10–11).

The story of the denials of Peter probably at one time was an independent narrative. Paul gives us a record of the Last Supper which he received of the Lord. It might have been an independent account, a parallel of similar records in the synoptic gospels.

For I received of the Lord that which also I delivered unto you, how that the Lord Jesus in the night in which he was betrayed took bread; and when he had given thanks, he brake it, and said, This is my body, which is for you: this do in remembrance of me. In like manner also the cup, after supper, saying, This cup is the new covenant in my blood: this do, as oft as ye drink it, in remembrance of me (1 Cor. xi, 23–25).

Every phrase of this except the opening sentence as far as the word " betrayed," is found in one or other of the Synoptic Gospels but Paul omits the thanksgiving over the cup and the giving of it with the accompanying words, the phrase " which is poured out for you," and also the words of Jesus, " I will not drink henceforth (or no more) of the fruit of the vine," etc. Now the phrases " In like manner," and " which is given for you: this do in remembrance of me," and " the new covenant " are found in Luke. The friendship of the Apostle with Luke, coupled with the closeness of the paralellism between the Pauline and Lucan accounts of the Institution of the Lord's Supper, suggests the possibility of an independent tradition known to them both, and if, as we shall see, Luke had a Passion Narrative of his own, it may be that the Lucan narrative was known to the Apostle.

In Luke, there are three possible independent
units, that of the Weeping Woman (xxiii, 27–31),
the Appearance of Jesus before Herod (xxiii, 6–12),
and the Penitent Thief (xxiii, 39–43), which are
all peculiar to the Gospel.   Of the scene before
.Herod, Dibelius thinks that it was interpolated into
the story because the friendship between Pilate
and Herod was read into Psalm ii, 1 ff. (p. 199).

Contents of the Primitive Narrative

Bultmann is of opinion that the oldest narrative
consisted of brief accounts of the Arrest, the Trials
and Condemnations by the Jewish courts and by
Pilate, the Way to the Cross, the Crucifixion and the
Death.   This view can be checked by what we find
in the New Testament, both in the Gospels and in
the contents of early Apostolic preaching (see p. 64).
The following are the main facts of the narrative
with letters against each to show that they are found
in Mark (M), Luke (L), John (J), and A (Apostolic
preaching).   Matthew is omitted because his
account is based on Mark.

The Treachery of Judas M. L. J (xiii, 2, 27, 30;
xviii, 2, 5). A (Acts i, 16).

The Last Supper   M. L. J (xiii, 2, 23–30).
A.

Gethsemane   M. L. J. (xviii, 1), A (Phil.
ii, 8 ; Hebrews v, 7f).

The Arrest   M. L. J. A. (Acts i, 16).

The Trial before the   M. L. J. A. (Acts ii, 23 ;
High Priests   iii, 13 f.).

The Roman Trial   M. L. J. A. (Acts iii, 13f ;
xiii, 27 f.).

Jesus before Herod   L. A. (Acts iv, 27).

The *Via Dolorosa*   M. L. J (xix, 17).
The Crucifixion and
  Death   M. L. J. A.
The Burial   M. L. J. A.

Thus Bultmann's views of the contents of the earliest Passion narrative is not inclusive enough; every main fact, even the *pericope* of Jesus before Herod, formed part of the teaching and preaching of the early Church.

Passion Narratives. That the fourth Evangelistic had access to special information is evident from the Gospel, but he has many points of contact with the Synoptic writers. Nearly every main section of the Passion story is illuminated by him, and if, as is very likely, he was acquainted with the gospels of Mark and Luke, the only reasonable explanation of the new material John has introduced within the main facts is that there was a Narrative with a special tradition associated with a great centre of Christianity, probably Ephesus. Below will be found the Johannine version with indications of its points of contact with the Marcan and Lucan versions.

When we turn to Mark's account, Dibelius thinks it is possible that traces of two versions can be discovered in it. This is based on the extreme difficulty of harmonizing the Marcan narrative. If Mark identified the Last Supper with the Passover, what is the meaning of Mark xiv, 1–2, which was quoted above? Dibelius holds that these verses could only make sense if the arrest took place before the feast of the Passover. He would also include with these verses the story of the Supper (xiv, 17–25), for in these verses the Supper is not called the Passover. This introduction and the preparation for the Supper are not part of the same story, since in it (xiv, 12–16) the Supper is definitely called " eating the passover " and in the upper room the two disciples " made ready the passover."   It is quite possible therefore, says Dibelius, that there was a tradition which told that Jesus was arrested after a supper eaten before His arrest which took place before the Jewish passover.   But if xiv, 12–16, is a separate legend which circulated independently in the oral period, its removal from the Marcan story is a possibility which cannot be overlooked. This would make Mark's chronology agree with that of John.   Let us consider this possibility.

One of the possible units is that of the Upper Room Furnished, which Dibelius calls a cult-Legend. If this story existed independently and if, with the Anointing, it was inserted into a Passion Narrative already in existence, some light is thrown on the complicated problem of the identification of the Last Supper with the Passover.   The removal of the section of five verses referring to the Upper Room (Mark xiv, 12–16) takes away from the Passion Narrative those particular passages which by using the terms, " eat the passover " (twice), " they prepared the passover," etc., identify the Supper with the Passover, and brings the Marcan story in line with that of the Fourth Gospel.   That is to say, the original Passion Narrative and the Johannine narrative will now agree that the Last Supper took place before the feast of the Passover, that Jesus was crucified when the paschal victims were being slain, and that Jesus rose from the dead on the day when the first-fruits were being presented in the temple.   Mark and John now agree with Paul who wrote, " Our passover also hath been sacrificed, even Christ " (1 Cor. v, 7), and " Now hath Christ been raised from the dead, the first fruit of them that are asleep " (1 Cor. xv, 20–23).

In this case, Mark xiv, 1–2, 10–11 will form not an independent Passion Narrative, as Dibelius thinks, but a part of the original Passion Narrative. Also the incident of the Upper Room Furnished will be a trace of the belief in some Christian circles that the Last Supper was to be identified with the Jewish Passover.

Has Luke an independent tradition ? In the Lucan story there are twelve variations in order as compared with Mark and the insertions of Marcan material has led to these variations. If the Marcan matter and certain probably scribal insertions are removed we get a complete version which is certainly non-Marcan. The complete list of insertions is as follows. Luke xxii, 18, 19–20, 22, 34, 42, 50b, 52b–53a, 54–62, 71 ; xxiii, 3, 17, 25, 26, 34b, 38, 44–45, 49, 50–53 (Redlich, pp. 99–105). We are now left with the independent Lucan Tradition. If from this we remove the Weeping Women, the scene before Herod, and the Penitent Thief which were probably isolated in tradition, we get what was probably the written narrative that was existent in Caesarea, a great centre of Christianity. These three incidents are bracketed in the text. As a stylist, he probably wrote up the original record without materially altering the substance of it. We begin at xxii, 47.

The Arrest

While he yet spake, behold, a multitude, and he that

was called Judas, one of the twelve, went before them; and he drew near unto Jesus to kiss him. But Jesus said unto him, Judas, betrayest thou the Son of man with a kiss? And when they that were about him saw what would follow, they said, Lord, shall we smite with the sword? And a certain one of them smote the servant of the high priest. But Jesus answered and said, Suffer ye thus far. And he touched his ear, and healed him. And Jesus said, This is your hour, and the power of darkness.

The Mocking

And the men that held Jesus mocked him, and beat him. And they blindfolded him, and asked him, saying, Prophesy: who is he that struck thee? And many other things spake they against him, reviling him.

The Hebrew Trial

And as soon as it was day, the assembly of the elders of the people was gathered together, both chief priests and scribes; and they led him away into their council, saying, If thou art the Christ, tell us. But he said unto them, If I tell you, ye will not believe: and if I ask *you*, ye will not answer. But from henceforth shall the Son of man be seated at the right hand of the power of God. And they all said, Art thou then the Son of God? And he said unto them, Ye say that I am.

The Roman Trial : before Herod

And the whole company of them rose up, and brought him before Pilate. And they began to accuse him, saying, We found this man perverting our nation, and forbidding to give tribute to Caesar, and saying that he himself is Christ a king. And Pilate said unto the chief priests and the multitudes, I find no fault in this man. But they were the more urgent, saying, He stirreth up the people, teaching throughout all Judaea, and beginning from Galilee even unto this place. But when Pilate heard it, he asked whether the man were a

Galilean. And when he knew that he was of Herod's jurisdiction, he sent him unto Herod, who himself also was at Jerusalem in these days.

[Now when Herod saw Jesus, he was exceeding glad: for he was of a long time desirous to see him, because he had heard concerning him; and he hoped to see some miracle done by him. And he questioned him in many words; but he answered him nothing. And the chief priests and the scribes stood, vehemently accusing him. And Herod with his soldiers set him at nought, and mocked him, and arraying him in gorgeous apparel sent him back to Pilate. And Herod and Pilate became friends with each other that very day: for before they were at enmity between themselves.]

And Pilate called together the chief priests and the rulers and the people, and said unto them, Ye brought unto me this man, as one that perverteth the people: and behold, I, having examined him before you, found no fault in this man touching those things whereof ye accuse him; no, nor yet Herod: for he sent him back unto us; and behold, nothing worthy of death hath been done by him. I will therefore chastise him, and release him. But they cried out all together, saying, Away with this man, and release unto us Barabbas: one who for a certain insurrection made in the city, and for murder, was cast into prison. And Pilate spake unto them again, desiring to release Jesus; but they shouted, saying, Crucify, crucify him. And he said unto them the third time, Why, what evil hath this man done? I have found no cause of death in him: I will therefore chastise him and release him. But they were instant with loud voices, asking that he might be crucified. And their voices prevailed. And Pilate gave sentence that what they asked for should be done.

The Daughters of Jerusalem

[And there followed him a great multitude of the people, and of women who bewailed and lamented him. But Jesus turning unto them said, Daughters of Jerusalem, weep not

for me, but weep for yourselves, and for your children.   For
behold, the days are coming, in which they shall say, Blessed
are the barren, and the wombs that never bare, and the breasts
that never gave suck.   Then shall they begin to say to the
mountains, Fall on us; and to the hills, Cover us.   For if
they do these things in the green tree what shall be done in
the dry?]

The Crucifixion

And there were also two others, malefactors, led with him
to be put to death.

And when they came unto the place which is called The
skull, there they crucified him, and the malefactors, one on
the right hand and the other on the left.   And Jesus said,
Father, forgive them; for they know not what they do.   And
the people stood beholding.   And the rulers also scoffed at
him, saying, He saved others; let him save himself, if this
is the Christ of God, his chosen.   And the soldiers also
mocked him, coming to him, offering him vinegar, and saying,
If thou art the King of the Jews, save thyself.

[And one of the malefactors which were hanged railed on
him, saying, Art not thou the Christ? save thyself and us.
But the other answered, and rebuking him said, Dost thou not
even fear God, seeing thou art in the same condemnation?
And we indeed justly; for we receive the due reward of our
deeds: but this man hath done nothing amiss.   And he said,
Jesus, remember me when thou comest in thy kingdom.
And he said unto him, Verily I say unto thee, To-day shalt
thou be with me in Paradise.]   And when Jesus had cried
with a loud voice, he said, Father, into thy hands I commend
my spirit: and having said this, he gave up the ghost.   And
when the centurion saw what was done, he glorified God,
saying, Certainly this was a righteous man.   And all the
multitudes that came together to this sight, when they beheld
the things that were done, returned smiting their breasts.

And it was the day of the Preparation, and the sabbath
drew on.

The Johannine tradition records or refers to every main event given by the Synoptists, the treachery of Judas, the Last Supper, Gethsemane, the Arrest, the Trials, the Denials of Peter, the *Via Dolorosa* and the Crucifixion. Omitting the Denials of Peter, the tradition is as given below, the points of contact (and they are many) being given within brackets. A passage of Dibelius is very much to the point, though we may question his opening words. " Since for him (St. John), not the death and the resurrection, but the ' going to the Father,' was the decisive event in salvation, a correct reproduction of the Passion story was really not to be expected. But since he nevertheless makes the report, and does so in relative agreement with the others, obviously the firmness and domination of the tradition determines him. The force of the events is so great that little room remains for an independent interpretation of the happenings " (p. 179).

In the text, verses which are O.T. quotations and others that are obviously redactional have been omitted. These are xviii, 9, 14, 32 ; xix, 20, 24b, 28. We begin at xviii, 1.

In Gethsemane

When Jesus had spoken these words, he went forth with his disciples (Mark xiv, 26, 32 ; Luke xxii, 39) over the brook Kidron, where was a garden, into which he entered, himself and his disciples. Now Judas also, which betrayed him, knew the place (Luke xxii, 40): for Jesus oft-times (Luke xxii, 39) resorted thither with his disciples.

The Arrest

Judas then, having received the band of soldiers, and officers from the chief priests (Mark xiv, 43) and the Pharisees, cometh thither with lanterns and torches and weapons (Mark xiv, 43). Jesus therefore, knowing all the things that were coming upon him, went forth, and saith unto them, Whom seek ye? They answered him, Jesus of Nazareth. Jesus saith unto them, I am he. And Judas also, which betrayed him (Mark xiv, 44) was standing with them. When therefore he said unto them, I am he, they went backward, and fell to the ground. Again therefore he asked them, Whom seek ye? And they said, Jesus of Nazareth. Jesus answered, I told you that I am he: if therefore ye seek me, let these go their way. Simon Peter therefore having a sword (Mark xiv, 47) drew it, and struck the high priest's servant (Mark xiv, 47; Luke xxii, 50) and cut off his right ear (Luke xxii, 50). Now the servant's name was Malchus. Jesus therefore said unto Peter, Put up the sword into the sheath: the cup (Mark xiv, 36; Luke xxii, 42) which the Father hath given me, shall I not drink it?

The Hebrew Trial

So the band, and the chief captain, and the officers of the Jews, seized (Luke xxii, 54) Jesus and bound him, and led him (Mark xiv, 53; Luke xxii, 54) to Annas first; for he was father in law to Caiaphas, which was high priest that year.

The high priest therefore asked Jesus of his disciples, and of his teaching. Jesus answered him, I have spoken openly to the world; I ever taught in synagogues, and in the temple, where all the Jews come together; and in secret spake I nothing. Why askest thou me? ask them that have heard me, what I spake unto them: behold, these know the things which I said. And when he had said this, one of the officers standing by struck Jesus (cf. Mark xiv, 65; Luke xxii, 63) with his hand, saying, Answerest thou the high priest so? Jesus answered him, If I have spoken evil, bear witness of the evil: but if well, why smitest thou me? Annas therefore sent him bound unto Caiaphas the high priest.

The Roman Trial

They lead Jesus therefore from Caiaphas into the palace (Mark xiv, 1 ; Luke xxiii, 1) ; and it was early (Mark xv, 1 ; Luke xxii, 66) ; and they themselves entered not into the palace (Mark xv, 16), that they might not be defiled, but might eat the passover. Pilate therefore went out unto them, and saith, What accusation bring ye against this man ? They answered and said unto him, If this man were not an evil-doer, we should not have delivered him up unto thee. Pilate therefore said unto them, Take him yourselves, and judge him according to your law. The Jews said unto him, It is not lawful for us to put any man to death.

Pilate therefore entered again into the palace, and called Jesus, and said unto him, Art thou the King of the Jews ? (Mark xv, 2 ; Luke xxiii, 3). Jesus answered, Sayest thou this of thyself, or did others tell it thee concerning me ? Pilate answered, Am I a Jew ? Thine own nation and the chief priests delivered thee unto me : what hast thou done ? Jesus answered, My kingdom is not of this world : if my kingdom were of this world, then would my servants fight, that I should not be delivered to the Jews : but now is my kingdom not from hence. Pilate therefore said unto him, Art thou a king then ? Jesus answered, Thou sayest (Mark xv, 2 ; Luke xxiii, 3) that I am a king. To this end have I been born, and to this end am I come into the world, that I should bear witness unto the truth. Everyone that is of the truth heareth my voice. Pilate saith unto him, What is truth ?

And when he had said this, he went out again unto the Jews, and saith unto them, I find no crime in him (Luke xxiii, 4, 14). But ye have a custom, that I should release unto you one at the passover (Mark xv, 6) : will ye therefore that I release unto you the King of the Jews ? (Mark xv, 9). They cried out therefore again, saying, Not this man, but Barabbas (Luke xxiii, 18 ; cf. Mark xv, 11). Now Barabbas was a robber (cf. Mark xv, 7 ; Luke xxiii, 19, 25a).

Then Pilate therefore took Jesus, and scourged him (Mark

xv, 15; cf. Luke xxiii, 16). And the soldiers plaited a crown of thorns, and put it on (Mark xv, 16 f.) his head, and arrayed him in a purple (Mark xv, 17) garment; and they came unto him, and said, Hail, King of the Jews! (Mark xv, 18) and they struck him with their hands (cf. Mark xv, 19). And Pilate went out again, and saith unto them, Behold, I bring him out to you, that ye may know that I find no crime in him (cf. Mark xv, 14; Luke xxiii, 22). Jesus therefore came out, wearing the crown of thorns and the purple garment. And Pilate saith unto them, Behold, the man! When therefore the chief priests and the officers saw him, they cried out, saying, Crucify him, crucify him (Luke xxiii, 21; cf. Mark xv, 13 f.). Pilate saith unto them, Take him yourselves, and crucify him: for I find no crime in him. The Jews answered him, We have a law, and by that law he ought to die, because he made himself the Son of God (Luke xxii, 70; cf. Mark xiv, 61). When Pilate therefore heard this saying, he was the more afraid; and he entered into the palace again, and saith unto Jesus, Whence art thou? But Jesus gave no answer. Pilate therefore saith unto him, Speakest thou not unto me? knowest thou not that I have power to release thee, and have power to crucify thee? Jesus answered him, Thou wouldest have no power against me, except it were given thee from above: therefore he that delivered me unto thee hath greater sin. Upon this Pilate sought to release him: but the Jews cried out, saying, If thou release this man, thou are not Caesar's friend: everyone that maketh himself a king (Luke xxiii, 2) speaketh against Caesar. When Pilate therefore heard these words, he brought Jesus out, and sat down on the judgment-seat at a place called the Pavement, but in Hebrew, Gabbatha. Now it was the Preparation of the Passover (Mark xiv, 15 f.): it was about the sixth hour (cf. Mark xv, 25; Luke xxiii, 44). And he saith unto the Jews, Behold, your King! They therefore cried out, Away with him, away with him (Luke xxiii, 18), crucify him (Luke xxiii, 21). Pilate saith unto them, Shall I crucify your King? The chief priests answered,

We have no king but Caesar. Then therefore he delivered him unto them to be crucified (Mark xv, 15; Luke xxiii, 25).

The Via Dolorosa and the Death

They took Jesus therefore: and he went out, bearing the cross for himself (cf. Mark xv, 21; Luke xxiii, 26), unto the place called The place of a skull (Mark xv, 22; Luke xxiii, 33) which is called in Hebrew Golgotha (Mark xv, 22); where they crucified him (Mark xv, 24; Luke xxiii, 33), and with him two others, on either side one, and Jesus in the midst (Mark xv, 27; Luke xxiii, 33). And Pilate wrote a title also, and put it on the cross. And there was written (cf. Mark xv, 26; Luke xxiii, 38), Jesus of Nazareth, the King of the Jews (Mark xv, 26; cf. Luke xxiii, 38). The chief priests of the Jews therefore said to Pilate, Write not, The King of the Jews; but, that he said, I am King of the Jews. Pilate answered, What I have written I have written.

The soldiers therefore, when they had crucified Jesus, took his garments, and made four parts, to every soldier a part; and also the coat: now the coat was without seam, woven from the top throughout. They said therefore one to another, Let us not rend it, but cast lots for it, whose it shall be (cf. Mark xv, 24; Luke xxiii, 34). These things therefore the soldiers did. But there were standing by the cross of Jesus his mother, and his mother's sister, Mary the wife of Clopas, and Mary Magdalene (Mark xv, 40). When Jesus therefore saw his mother, and the disciple standing by, whom he loved, he saith unto his mother, Woman, behold thy son ! Then saith he to the disciple, Behold, thy mother ! And from that hour the disciple took her unto his own home.

After this Jesus saith, I thirst. There was set there a vessel full of vinegar: so they put a sponge full of vinegar (Mark xv, 36; cf. Luke xxiii, 36) upon hyssop, and brought it to his mouth. When Jesus therefore had received the vinegar, he said, It is finished: and he bowed his head, and gave up his spirit (Mark xv, 37; Luke xxiii, 46).

In Matthew, which is based on Mark, there are a few additions inserted into the Marcan text, as well as a few independent *pericopae*. In the Agony in the Garden we find it stated that Jesus " prayed a third time, saying again the same words " (xxvi, 44). Also that Jesus said to one of them " that were with Jesus,"

Put up again thy sword into its place: for all they that take the sword shall perish with the sword. Or thinkest thou that I cannot beseech my Father, and he shall even now send me more than twelve legions of angels? How then should the scriptures be fulfilled, that thus it must be (xxvi, 52–54).

Also two legends :

So when Pilate saw that he prevailed nothing, but rather that a tumult was arising, he took water, and washed his hands before the multitude, saying, I am innocent of the blood of this righteous man : see ye to it. And all the people answered and said, His blood be on us, and on our children (xxvii, 24 f.).

And the earth did quake; and the rocks were rent; and the tombs were opened; and many bodies of the saints that had fallen asleep were raised; and coming forth out of the tombs after his resurrection they entered into the holy city and appeared unto many (xxvii, 51 f.).

To these must be added two stories of Judas (xxvi, 14–16, xxvii, 3–10) which may be historical.

Thus we conclude that there are certainly three Passion Narratives in the Gospels and indications of a fourth in Mark.

The Passion Narrative and the O.T. A Passion Narrative, in order to prove that the Messiah had to die that he might redeem both Jew and Gentile, would require evidence that the death of the Messiah was according to Scripture. Hence the frequent references to passages in the Old Testament which substantiated what had actually happened so closely that quotations would at times be used to describe actual occurrences. For instance both Mark and Luke use Psalm xxii, 19, not as a quotation but as a form of words which adequately conveyed the course of an event. "They part his garments among them casting lots." So also in the use of phrases like "wine mingled with myrrh" and "wagging their heads." Words from the Old Testament were on our Lord's lips on the Cross. "A Bible word on the lips of a dying man means a religious reverence for the Bible, and, in any case union with God." The cry of dereliction "in no case expressed a doubting sense of abandonment, for to quote from the Bible is always a proof of faith" (Dibelius, p. 194). The Passion of Jesus was found depicted in the Old Testament (Psalm xxii, 7, 18; xxxi, 22; lxix, 3, 9, 21; Isaiah l, 6; liii, 12) and in this way it was evident proof that the Passion was in accordance with the will of God. The events of the Passion were foretold by Scripture and therefore had soteriological significance. Only in one case had a quotation been doubted as expressing a historical fact. This is in the sum of thirty pieces of silver paid as blood money to Judas (Zech. xi, 12 f.). Matthew quoted the words and gave the wrong context for he assigns them to Jeremiah (Matt. xxvii, 9).

THE RESURRECTION NARRATIVES

Whilst the Passion Narrative was in earliest days given in continuous form, there is no evidence that similar treatment was accorded to the Resurrection.

M

The Appearances of Jesus after He rose from the dead are independent self-contained stories and, unlike the Passion, cannot be fitted into an orderly narrative.   The accounts in the Gospels differ and give us differing cycles of events, one in Galilee, the other in Jerusalem.   The evidence of Paul gives a bare list which is probably confined to events in Jerusalem (1 Cor. xv, 4–7).   Luke's account suggests that the appearances to the two disciples on the way to Emmaus, to Simon (xxiv, 34) and to the Apostles was followed the same day by the Ascension.   The Marcan narrative is only a fragment, and the references to Galilee in xiv, 28, " After I am raised up, I will go before you into Galilee " and in the message of a young man[1] in the tomb " Go, tell his disciples and Peter, He goeth before you into Galilee : there shall ye see him, as he said unto you " (xvi, 7) indicate that the last ending probably gave an account of an appearance to Peter and other Apostles in Galilee.

Two conclusions may be drawn from the disconnected nature of these traditions.   The first is that, as Mark tells us, the story of the Empty Grave (xvi, 1–8) was part of the oldest primitive tradition. That it was a *pericope* may be indicated by the names given at the beginning of the story, which repeat names given in the previous verse (xv, 47).   The repetition would have been ordinarily superfluous. The Empty Grave was in primitive tradition evidence of the actual Resurrection of Jesus.   If the legendary account of the actual Resurrection in the *Gospel of Peter* existed in tradition, the primitive Church discarded it as being pure imagination for the

---

[1] Was he Mark?   The same Greek word is used here as in Mark xiv, 51.

sounder and purer historical evidence of the Empty
Grave.

The second conclusion that may be drawn is that
in the earliest days there was no clamant need for
an ordered Resurrection narrative.   Eye-witnesses
could testify to having seen Jesus after His Resurrection, and there were hundreds of them (1 Cor.
xv, 7).   The fact of the tremendous happening on
Easter Day was assured by first-hand evidence of an
indisputable character.   It could therefore raise no
difficulty. The Passion however did raise a problem.
Had the problem not existed the story of the Passion
would have consisted mainly of independent units,
as with the stories of the ministry and of the Resurrection.   This problem was the problem of the
Cross.   Why was it necessary that the Messiah
should suffer ignominious shame and death?   The
answer could only be given by an account of the
Passion supported by references to the inspired
writings of the Old Testament.

Whatever problems, therefore, may be raised by
the Resurrection, Form Criticism has brought us
nearer to the events of Easter Day by the support it
gives to the assurance that Jesus was visibly seen
and spoken to and recognized by disciples—" The
story of Emmaus has been preserved in an almost
pure form" (Dibelius, p. 191)—that the list given by
Paul is a list which was in circulation in early days
as a piece of written tradition, and that the Empty
Grave circulated in earliest days as a single unit
amongst other stories of the Resurrection.

CHAPTER VII

FORMLESS STORIES

THE title of this chapter has been deliberately chosen, for whilst the Apothegm-Stories and the Miracle-Stories possess structural forms, the other stories in the Gospel possess no form whatsoever. Form Criticism therefore has nothing to do with a mass of stories in the Gospels. For example what common form can be perceived in the stories of the Confession of Peter, the Entry into Jerusalem, the Transfiguration, and Jesus in the temple at the age of twelve?

The only contribution made by Form Criticism to the study of these stories is that they circulated in the main as independent units. There are cases where they were possibly handed down in pairs, as in the stories of the Upper Room Furnished and the Finding of the Ass, or in larger groups as in the Temptation narratives (but see p. 103). Now apart from the Stories of the Birth, Passion and Resurrection of Jesus there are less than forty other narratives. That there were others in tradition which were not placed on record is a certainty, just as we know that many sayings of Jesus did not find mention in the Gospel narratives.

The terms used by Form Critics for stories other than those possessing form are Legenda and Mythen, which can be translated into English by Legend and Myth respectively. The terms are unsuitable for English students for they designate that which is unhistorical. Bultmann, the extreme Form Critic, says outright that by legends he means those narratives which are untrustworthy. But Dibelius is not so extravagant in summarily disposing of the stories of the Gospels. By the term Legend he means a religious story about a saintly man or woman. Dibelius further distinguishes between Legend and Myth, and confines the latter term to a story which introduces supernatural beings. However, whatever be the historical value of Legends and Myths, they possess no form; any title given to them can only designate the nature of the contents. They are stories with this difference, that the main interest in some of them may lie in others than Jesus, though Jesus comes into the narrative. This is a matter for further consideration but before this is done some fuller reference must be made to the views of two Form Critics.

Bultmann argues that Legends have a form because they are all cultic, that is to say, they possess a form suitable for purposes of worship. He does not therefore use the term to define any narrative " form " but only a function. The cultic interest is to be seen in the Last Supper. The Sacrament was thought to have originated in that meal and so the narrative was transformed into a cult-legend. Similar treatment was given to " the undoubted fact " that Jesus was baptized by John. The Transfiguration and the Confession of Peter are probably Resurrection narratives which were all composed in the interest of faith and under an active Christian imagination, and so on. The whole argument is so subjective and so influenced not by the imagination of the community but by that of the author that he loses the sympathy of any who desire to find a

substratum of truth in it.   When it is recalled that
he found the narrative portions of his Apothegms
unreliable in the main and held that the Miracle-
Stories were unhistorical, and classes nearly all the
rest of the narrative in the same category, it is not
surprising that to him the figure and Personality of
Jesus are very faint and unsubstantial.

That legendary stories exist in the Gospel of St.
Matthew was realized by English scholars before
the advent of Form Criticism.   The Resurrection
of Saints, Peter Walking on the Sea, the Stater in
the Fish's mouth, were admitted to be legends.
Others felt that the miraculous escape of Jesus in
Nazareth (Luke iv, 29 f.), Pilate's Wife's Dream and
probably the Cursing of the Fig Tree were legends or
included legendary traits.   Further popular tales
were held to be exemplified in the Gerasene Demoniac and the Death of John the Baptist.   Thus
English scholarship has proceeded with caution and
restraint. Here it may claim the support of Dibelius.

Legends, says Dibelius, are " religious narratives
of saintly men " in the way we speak of the Legends
of Saints.   They satisfy the need of knowing something about the holy men and women who were with
Jesus and of knowing Jesus Himself.   " A legendary form as such is in any case no decisive objection
against the historicity of the hero or even of an
event " (p. 109). Thus while the term Legend
does not exclude historical traits, the main interest
does not lie in the question of trustworthiness but
in the sanctity of the hero.   Now the typical motif in
Legends is that of self-deliverance, as in the *Gospel
of Thomas*.   But there is only one instance of it in
the Evangelical tradition, namely in the escape at

Nazareth (Luke iv, 29 f.). The Temptation cannot be another, for Jesus refuses self-deliverance.

There is one other admission which Dibelius makes. The Legends are clearly in his view interested not in Jesus but in secondary things and persons. " Hence in this case analysis cannot prove the type by examples as in Paradigms and Novellen " (p. 132). In other words, the stories of the Gospels apart from the Paradigms and Miracle-Stories have no structural form. They are form-less narrative units of oral tradition.

Thus Dibelius, though he uses the term Legend in a literary sense, is conscious of the fact that the historical problem is a possible matter for inquiry. His discussion of Legends moves from the literary sense to the historical as he searches for the original form of a Legend, that is, the form it might have had in the oral period. A similar problem came up when the number of possible Apothegm-Stories was discussed. For example, Did the story of the Sons of Zebedee include a mention of their names? If it did, says Dibelius, the story is not in its original form. Again, Is the story of Martha and Mary a Legend or a Paradigm? He thinks it was a Legend, since in his opinion the interest in the narrative is in the two sisters. Whether the interest lay in Jesus or in His followers is not of importance, so long as it is clear that we are dealing with all narrative stories in the Gospels, which are not Apothegm-Stories and Miracle-Stories, and are not part of the Passion narrative. These Form-less Stories may be arranged in two groups :

1. Stories of Jesus and His disciples.
2. Stories of Jesus and supernatural beings.

STORIES OF JESUS AND HIS DISCIPLES

These formless stories, we have repeatedly stated, stand outside the purview of Form Criticism. But since Form Critics have applied terms to them which throw doubt on their trustworthiness, the charge of falsity must be considered and that only in general terms. It can be shown that these formless narratives are not devoid of historical value, and that even the so-called Myths enshrine facts of mystical experience. A conversion or the conquest of a temptation is no less a fact because it has taken place in a man's inner consciousness. The conversion of Saul had a greater influence in the world's history than the discovery of America or the conquest of the Spanish Armada.

In Mark. We are left with the following seventeen stories. The Preaching of John the Baptist (i, 4–8), the Baptism of Jesus (i, 9–11), the Temptation (i, 12–13), the Call of the first Disciples (i, 16–20), the Retirement into a Desert (i, 35–39), the Call of Levi (ii, 13–14), the Appointment of the Twelve (iii, 13–19), the Mission of the Apostles (vi, 7, 30), Herod and Jesus (vi, 14–16), the Death of John the Baptist (vi, 17–29), the Syro-Phoenician Woman (vii, 24–29), the Leaven of the Pharisees (viii, 14–21), the Confession of Peter (viii, 27–30), the Transfiguration (ix, 2–8), the Finding of the Ass (xi, 1–6), the Entry into Jerusalem (xi, 7–10), the Upper Room Furnished (xiv, 12–16).

The Baptism, the Temptation and the Transfiguration will come under our second group and are best taken together because of their mystical character.

Of the other fourteen stories, that of John the

Baptist and his preaching is significant in that it
begins the Marcan Gospel and in this respect
corresponds with the conditions laid down by Peter
for the choice of an Apostle (Acts i, 21). The
connection of Peter with the Gospel is thus implied
at the very beginning of it. Petrine reminiscences
are clearly to be seen in other sections which follow
the Temptation. The Calling of the Apostles is an
illustration. The detail there is suggestive. Simon
and Andrew are in shallow water and Jesus, as He
passes by, can speak to them easily. Then comes a
contrast, for after the incident is completed by the
response of the brothers, there is a second independent incident, the call of James and John.
They are in deep water, a little distance from the
shore and Jesus " calls " them, that is, hails them.
Jesus speaks to one pair and calls loudly to the other.
The eye-witness has further noticed with interest
the hired servants who were present with their father.
These unusual details can only have been given by a
careful observer, undoubtedly Peter. Again, in
the Retirement into a Desert Place at the end of a
series of events in a day spent at Capernaum (see
p. 38), a word in the story is striking evidence of
personal observation and participation. Jesus leaves
the house early in the morning, unknown to Peter.
When His absence is discovered, Peter and others
" track " Him down—a very illuminating word.
The presence of an eye-witness, undoubtedly Peter,
is evident.

Of the Call of Levi, little need be said except that
no objection has been raised to it as a fact. The
only point raised has been the locale of the feast.
Mark and Matthew probably imply that it was

Peter's house; Luke however definitely says it was the home of Levi. This call is in keeping with the historical tradition of our Lord's friendship with publicans, and the controversies to which that friendship gave rise.

The Appointment of the Twelve is given by each of the Synoptists, and each gives a different version. The order of the names varies in each and there is an uncertainty in the name of one of them. Again the order varies in Acts i, 13, and in John xxi, where we read of Peter first, then Thomas, then Nathanael and lastly "the sons of Zebedee." It is evident therefore that traditions existed in various centres of Christianity, that each tradition was independent, and that all the traditions did not agree. In short, there is every reason to accept the fact of the selection and appointment of the Twelve.

The Mission of the Twelve may or may not be identified with the Lucan Mission of the Seventy. The interest in the Mission and the charge to the Twelve would have been of profound interest to the early Church in their missionary work. It is the personal touch we are searching for. We find it in the narrative in Mark, in the mention of the kind of money the Apostles were not to carry in their cummerbund. Mark says copper money which is all the Apostles were evidently meant to have, whereas Luke and Matthew bring in silver and gold. Now Peter in the story of the Lame Man at the Beautiful Gate admits that he had no silver and gold (Acts iii, 6). The coincidence is remarkable and shows that the Marcan narrative is primitive.

The incident of Herod and Jesus is recorded by all of the Synoptists with slight variations, of which the most striking is that referring to the Baptist. In Mark, Herod says, " John, whom I beheaded, he is risen " ; in Luke, the utterance reads, " John I beheaded : but who is this, about whom I hear such things? " In Mark's account, Jesus is identified with John risen from the dead. The popular explanation of the miracles worked by Jesus was that the resurrection of John enabled him to have that power, and the superstition was accepted by the Tetrarch. The attitude of Herod is quite primitive and was the talk of the court. This incident and the story of the Baptist's death are picturesque and read like popular accounts of common talk and rumour. But that does not mean they are unhistorical in the basic fact of the death of the Baptist at the hands of Herod Antipas.

The Syro-Phoenician woman is of interest for whilst Mark states that it was the apt and ready retort of the woman which won Christ's favour and help, Matthew says it was the faith of the woman. The Marcan narrative is probably based on a more primitive Apothegm-Story of the incident (see p. 98). Mark's term " by race " suggests that the woman knew Greek and that Jesus spoke to her in that language.

The Confession of Peter is not accepted as historical by Form Critics since they adopt Wrede's theory of the Messianic Secret. To Bultmann it is unhistorical. Dibelius says that it " cannot be regarded forthwith " as a Legend but in Matthew " it has become a typical Legend, name-giving and *vaticinium ex eventu* included " (p. 115).

The Entry into Jerusalem given in Mark raises no historical difficulties though Matthew through a misunderstanding of Zachariah (ix, 9) makes out that there were two animals, the ass and the foal, whereas he should have read it as referring to one animal.

The Finding of the Upper Room and the Finding of the Ass are called by Dibelius " Cult Legends." In the former he sees a miracle, "Divine provision takes care that the cultus is rightly carried out." The Christian meal is a continuation of the Passover and it is important to know how Jesus had celebrated the meal. There need not, however, be a miracle in the Finding if there is anything in the tradition that the house where the supper was held is to be identified with the house of Mary, the mother of Mark. It may have been Mark who played the part of the goodman of the house in the story. Luke gives the names of the two disciples as Peter and John. The third Evangelist thus recognized in the Marcan narrative a Petrine reminiscence. As for the Finding of the Ass, says Dibelius, " the motives of prophesied meeting and of miraculous direction " connects it with the Finding of the Upper Room. But need it be miraculous? Jesus had friends in Jerusalem and we cannot assume that no visit had been paid by Him to the city before the Triumphal Entry. However, apart from this question of prevision, Dibelius considers the whole of Mark xi, 1–10, a cultus-legend " since it is not the holy Person of Jesus but the holy word of the Old Testament, read aloud in the cultus, which determines the whole " (p. 122). Of the historicity of the event, apart from the Messianic significance in it, he is not doubtful.

The Leaven of the Pharisees is too obscure for

discussion. This is stressed by Matthew who explains that Jesus was not referring to bread but to the teaching of the Pharisees and Sadducees.

In Luke's Gospel. We find left us, Jesus and the Doctors in the Temple (ii, 41–52), the Visit to Nazareth (iv, 16–30), the Call of Simon (v, 1–11), the Sinful Woman in Simon's House (vii, 36–50), The Women Disciples (viii, 1–3), the Samaritan Village (ix, 52b–56), Martha and Mary (x, 38–42), Zacchaeus (xix, 1–10), and probably the Rejoicing of the Disciples (xix, 39–40), and the Weeping over Jerusalem (xix, 41–44).

Jesus in the Temple is not the story of a precocious boy, nor does it represent Him as omniscient. He is a boy keen to learn by listening to the Rabbis and asking them questions. He is not represented as being conscious of the Messiahship but as being at home in the heavenly Father's house. The beautiful story reads true.

The Visit to Nazareth is fuller in Luke than in Mark. It is probable that Luke obtained the additional details from the family of Jesus. Dibelius thinks that the basis of the Marcan story may be a Paradigm and it is regarded as an Apothegm-Story in this book. The sayings about Sarepta and Naaman need not be interpolations; the references would leave an indelible impression on the minds of Jewish hearers. The conclusion of the Lucan story with its miraculous escape may however be redactional.

The Call of Simon has often been held to be a combination of the Marcan story and of John xxi, 1–14, or even a doublet of the latter. Dibelius does not think the story was based on Mark because

it says nothing about " fishers of men," and says
that the story from verse 4 may be a Legend of
Simon, the earlier verses being added by Luke.
Also, true to his definition of a Legend, Dibelius
says that the story may preserve a historical
fact of the connection of a catch with a call. The
miraculous draught can be rationalized easily.
Jesus observed, what no one else noticed, a shoal
of fish, with which the Sea of Galilee abounded in
certain places and conditions. He was thus able
to advise where the net should be cast.

The stories of the Sinful Woman in Simon's
House, of the Samaritan Village, Martha and Mary
and Zacchaeus have been dealt with in a previous
chapter (see pp. 107 ff.). The Women Disciples
shows Luke's interest in women. The Rejoicing
of Disciples and the Weeping over Jerusalem may
be sayings proper with artificial introductions (see
p. 109).

When we survey these stories in Mark and Luke,
certain inferences can be drawn. There are not
quite thirty of them, to which of course must be
added the narratives in the Apothegm-Stories and
the Johannine stories. The total is by no means
large, and this may imply a lack of a literary biographical interest. This is not surprising among
" unliterary men "—to use a term favoured by
Dibelius. The early Church would preserve those
narratives which helped them to solve the special
problems which arose in their new circumstances.
The importance of what were preserved is that in
them we find stories connected with the critical
stages of the Ministry, the preaching of John, the
choice of the Twelve, the Rejection in Nazareth,

the Retreat outside Galilee, the Transfiguration and the final journey to Jerusalem.

Secondly, we notice that Dibelius was justified in calling attention to the interest of the primitive communities in holy men and women. The early Church did long to know about Simon, James and John, Levi, Martha and Mary, Mary Magdalene, the relatives of Jesus, Bartimaeus and so on. Mere lists of Apostles and mere names of disciples were unsatisfying. There must have been, and very naturally, a personal interest in men and women who were closely attached to Jesus.

Thirdly, like human beings of ordinary kind, the early Christians took an interest in retaining and retailing popular tales which were connected with Jesus and John the Baptist. The naturalness and picturesqueness of the few such stories in the Gospels would appeal to the oriental mind.

Fourthly, the evidence borne by the Marcan stories to the presence of eye-witnesses is too strong to be neglected. If, as Dibelius believes, Paradigms existed early in the history of the Church when eye-witnesses were present, the same might be said of many of the Legends.

Lastly, the Lucan stories possess special characteristics. They portray Jesus as tender with women (names of those who ministered to Him being retained), Jesus as One who possessed a universalistic aspect towards nations, Jesus as the great Admirer of domestic happiness and home life, Jesus as the Friend of the under-dog.

In John we find a few stories, the Call of Nathanael (i, 45–51), Nicodemus (iii, 1–21), Jesus and John (iii, 22–30), the Woman at the Well (iv, 1–42), the

Inquiry of the Greeks (xii, 20–22), the Feet-Washing (xiii, 4–10), the Visits to Jerusalem at the feasts of the Tabernacles and of the Dedication (vii, 1–13; x, 22–42). We omit here the Miracles, the Anointing and the Cleansing of the Temple, the last two containing parallels in the Synoptists.

That in the majority, if not all, of these eight stories the foundation of each is an historical event would be admitted by all but the most sceptical. That the author is dealing with the events symbolically and doctrinally would be admitted by all but believers in verbal inspiration. The view here taken is that in every case there is a basis of fact and that the Evangelist allegorizes history and dramatizes in allegorical form, and that the attribution of the Messiahship to Jesus in the popular sense early in the Gospel may probably be historical.

The Call of Nathanael is the final event in a series of calls, the first being of two disciples of John the Baptist. Andrew, Philip and Nathanael in turn confess that Jesus is the Messiah. Simon, who does not do so in words, is to be given the name Cephas, at some future date, which is not specified. That a Legend of Nathanael lies behind the call is acknowledged by Dibelius (p. 117). The Visit of Nicodemus is not impossible as an actual event, for he was intimately connected with the burial of Jesus. The anxiety of John's disciples for their leader's position and prestige is more than likely.

The story of the Woman at the Well is very clearly the dramatic setting of an historical fact. That the disciples found him speaking to a woman is pure history, but the conversation with the woman is probably in the main an interpretation. If this estimate of the story is correct, there is no reason to attribute clairvoyant knowledge to Jesus. The " five husbands " has been held to be no more than a symbolic reference to the past religious history of the Samaritans (cf. 2 Kings xvii, 30 f.), but this is doubtful.

Another dramatic arrangement is probably to be seen in the Inquiry of the Greeks. The Evangelist is so set on his interpretation of the event that he does not give us any information whether or not the Greeks saw Jesus.

We are left with the two Visits to Jerusalem, which may be true history for they can be fitted into Mark's chronology, and the incident of the Feet-Washing by Jesus. This last follows soon on the incident of Mary's washing of our Lord's feet. This arrangement may have been deliberate. Doubt has been thrown on the incident as being an artificial creation of the author. Others, e.g. Goguel in his *Life of Jesus*, see in the incident an allegory of the Last Supper. That allegorical traits exist in the narrative is evident. It is so in the conversation between Jesus and Peter. But whether the whole story of the Feet-Washing is an allegory of the Last Supper and has replaced it is doubtful.

No one will care to dogmatize when the Fourth Gospel is discussed. Fact and interpretation are so closely interwoven that they cannot always be distinguished. But this is not to say that Fact is not one of the elements of the Gospel.

In Matthew there are very few stories which are non-Marcan and of these we have accepted some as legends (see p. 182). The Centurion's Servant and the Message of John from prison and the Temple

N

Tax of the Half-Shekel are amongst the Apothegm-
Stories. It is however interesting to note that
Matthew might have known an independent cycle
of Petrine stories, which included the Confession,
the Walking on the Sea and the Stater.

JESUS AND THE SUPERNATURAL WORLD

Form Criticism has no special contribution to
make to the stories of the Birth and Infancy of Jesus
except that they were at one time independent
stories. The historical value varies between scepticism and a basis of fact. "Whether they were
historical or unhistorical, we cannot say" writes
the conservative Dibelius. In fact he admits that
in them are traditions of the Church and "these
ideas have no fundamental significance for the
Form-geschichte of the Gospel, because they are
subject to other laws than the mass of Gospel
tradition" (p. 123).

We may accept that judgment, but add to it that
these stories represent, at times in poetical form and
at times in symbolic form, the conception of the
primitive Church that Jesus was divine and was
Messiah, Saviour and God, proclaimed by the
angels, foretold by the prophets and acknowledged
by men and women of saintly character and purity
of heart.

We must now consider the Baptism, the Temptation and the Transfiguration.

The Baptism of Jesus was an undoubted fact
even to Bultmann. Dibelius only calls it a myth
because the revelation from heaven was originally
for Jesus and not for John the Baptist. By myth
he means "a many-sided inter-action between

mythological but not human beings "—mythological being contrasted with human. Luke, he points out, turns the Marcan story into a personal Legend, and Matthew into an Epiphany. Jesus did not reveal the experience to others ; had he done so, the section would have been preserved as a word of Jesus. The baptism is historical and in this way the event is not a pure myth.

That the Marcan account is primitive may be seen by the absence of any reference to the hesitation of John to baptize Jesus. Matthew's version is apologetic for he has to explain why Jesus, though He was sinless, was baptized. Why then do Form Critics call the Marcan account mythical? They are obsessed with the theory of the Messianic secret, and the accounts of Mark and of Q can be interpreted to mean that the Messianic consciousness of Jesus was a secret known in the beginning to Jesus alone. For Mark's account describes a subjective experience of Jesus. He alone saw the heavens rent asunder, saw the Holy Spirit as a dove, heard the heavenly Voice. This mystical experience in Matthew and Luke becomes objective, if not materialistic.

The Sojourn in the Wilderness, as a matter of pure fact, cannot be gainsaid. Each of the Synoptists has an independent tradition, shown by the variations in the three accounts (Redlich, p. 46). The three temptations however are subjective experiences of a mystical character probably at various crises of the Ministry, the first in the Wilderness, the offer of the Crown after the Feeding of the multitude, and the Pinnacle temptation on the way to Jerusalem (see p. 104) or when Jesus rebuked

N*

Simon Peter and said to him, " Get thee behind me, Satan : for thou mindest not the things of God, but the things of men " (Mark viii, 33).

The Transfiguration too was a mystical experience. Some scholars think it was probably an experience not of Jesus but of Peter. Matthew calls it a vision, which does not mean a hallucination. Peter after a severe mental strain lasting six days during which he was mentally perplexed with the appalling horror of the Messiah's approaching suffering and death experienced the vision. " Interpreted in this way the vision of the Transfiguration is in line with a very real and influential type of psychical experi- ence "[1] such as befell Saul on the way to Damascus, or Constantine in his vision of the Cross, or Joan of Arc in her vision of the Virgin—three visions which have in an extraordinary way influenced and deter- mined the course of history. We may question this explanation, but not the importance of the event as a turning point in the history of the ministry. It was a fact that, on the Mount, Jesus had a mystical experience of great moment in the story of the Cross. It was one which, with the Baptism and the Temp- tation, was a crisis in our Lord's life.

.   .   .   .   .

Thus we end our study with thoughts of spiritual experience. The Form-less stories, even those called myths, bear their witness to the reality of the Cross and of the Personality of Jesus. Form Criticism has failed to diminish the splendour and the reality of the divine Jesus, who is the Christ of history. We still see Him, not as One whose form is

[1] H. D. A. Major in *The Mission and Message of Jesus*, pp. 113 ff.

" for the most part hidden from us," not as One of whom we hear " little more than a whisper of His voice," but as He really was in the hearts and minds of those who were eye-witnesses and ministers of the word—the Jesus who went about doing good and spake, as no man ever spake, with such power that those who followed Him turned the world upside down and would gladly have died for Him.

BIBLIOGRAPHY

A. W. F. BLUNT: *The Gospels and the Critics.*

R. BULTMANN: **The Study of the Synoptic Gospels* in F. C. Grant's *Form Criticism.*
Jesus and the Word.

F. C. BURKITT: *The Gospel History and its Transmission.*
Jesus Christ.

C. F. BURNEY: *The Poetry of our Lord.*

A. T. CADOUX: *The Sources of the Second Gospel.*

M. DIBELIUS: **From Tradition to Gospel*, translated by B. L. Woolf.
Fresh Approach to the New Testament.
Gospel Criticism and Christology.

C. H. DODD: **The Parables of the Kingdom.*
The Apostolic Preaching.
The Present Task in New Testament Studies.
The Framework of the Gospel Narrative in the *Expository Times*, June 1932.

B. S. EASTON: **The Gospel before the Gospels.*
Christ in the Gospels.

F. C. GRANT: *Form Criticism.*
The Growth of the Gospels.

HOSKYNS and DAVEY: *The Riddle of the New Testament.*

R. H. LIGHTFOOT: **History and Interpretation in the Gospels.*

T. W. MANSON: **The Teaching of Jesus.*

MAJOR, MANSON and WRIGHT: *The Mission and Message of Jesus.*

H. D. A. MAJOR: *Jesus by an Eye Witness.*

PEAKE'S Commentary: Supplement to
A. E. J. RAWLINSON :   *The Gospel according to St. Mark.*
E. B. REDLICH :   **The Student's Introduction to the Synoptic Gospels.*
VINCENT TAYLOR :   **The Formation of the Gospel Tradition.*
                        The Gospels.

INDEX OF REFERENCES

INDEX OF SUBJECTS